# Singapore to London by Rail

## Slow Travel Adventures

by

**TJW Thornes**

WASH HOUSE PUBLISHING

Travel

Published by Wash House Publishing 2022

Printed on demand by CPI Group.
The CPI Group is committed to the prevention of
pollution and continual improvement to reduce our
effect on the environment.

**ISBN 978-1-7391357-2-0**

# Contents

# Acknowledgements

This book is in two parts: the real story of an overland journey from Singapore to London in part 1; and a mostly fictional 'Slow Travel' account in part 2. Neither of these travelogues – the factual nor the fictional – would have come about without the help of some key sources of information. For would-be globe-trotters by train, you can't go far wrong asking advice from the Man in Seat 61, whom I would like to thank for his excellent website (www.seat61.com), which helped immeasurably when it came to planning my route. A number of travel agencies were also useful for booking tickets and arranging visas, especially Real Russia (www.realrussia.co.uk), and I am indebted to their Beijing office for being so helpful in arranging for me to collect my Trans-Siberian tickets late. Were it not for the kindness of the person in that office, I might have been delayed for a week at considerable expense! I would also like to thank the Royal Society for permitting me to attend their conference in the first place.

For Part 2, I thank the commissioning editors of The Poor Print newspaper (www.thepoorprint.com), in which the largely fictional travelogue was originally published. In particular, Jacob Warn, Alex Waygood and Aidan Chivers are responsible for encouraging my imaginary wanderings and putting them into print. My thanks to you all.

T J W Thornes
22nd August 2022

# SINGAPORE TO LONDON BY RAIL

## A 16-DAY ADVENTURE

*A true account of a journey taken in June 2017*

# Singapore to London by Land:
## A 16-day Adventure
### *Introduction*

In June 2017, I was fortunate enough to be able to attend the Royal Society Commonwealth Science Conference, a four-yearly event for scientists to gather from across the British Commonwealth. Being as I was mid-way through a doctorate in environmental physics, this seemed to me to be a fantastic way of meeting other scientists from a diverse range of disciplines and share my own research. Indeed, there are few things that scientists like more than to meet together and take a look at what everyone else has been doing. The chance to go to a conference this big doesn't come along often, and I was loathe to let it pass me by.

Yet there was just one problem: it was taking place on the island of Singapore, essentially on the other side of the world from where I was based in Oxford. And, being a passionate environmentalist, flying was not something I was eager to do. The answer to my quandary was, of course, the train, and with the help of various sources of priceless information about the overland route to Asia, a potential hiccup was turned into the journey of a lifetime.

Yes, I took the aeroplane on the way there – the ticket had already been bought for me by the conference organisers – and hated every minute of those fourteen hours trapped inside a pressurised metal capsule. Soaring far above the land and sea, almost oblivious to what's beneath, while at the same time belching out pollutants that could help to destroy everything worth seeing anyway is not my idea of fun. But I took the train on the way back – and enjoyed every minute spent meeting countless people across a whole host of fascinating places over the sixteen days it took me to get home.

This is the story of those sixteen days, with all their twists and turns, setbacks and resolutions. If nothing else, it proves that the journey can be done – and doesn't take as long as some might be inclined to think. It should be borne in mind by the reader that I do not, and did not at the time, possess a mobile 'phone. Once out on the rails, I was completely on my own – apart from the often very helpful and interesting strangers I found myself sharing parts of my journey with of course. There was no means of changing course on-route. I simply had to trust that the connections I had booked or expected to run would be there.

It was a risk, but one well worth taking. As I travelled, I kept a diary of all that occurred on the trip. This is the story of that trip, only sparsely edited from my original notes.

## Day 1: Singapore to Kuala Lumpur
### *Saturday 17th June*

*The Slow Train*: Ready to board at Johar Bahru station

I awoke at 5.30 in Singapore, where I had been for just a few days, and soon was on my way to Clementi MRT (Mass Rapid Transit) station to catch a quiet train to Woodlands – with views of the alluring jungle region of Singapore on the way – where the next adventure, madness it sometimes seemed, was to begin. I was to travel back to the UK, half way around the world, not by plane but by bus and train. My hope was that all the connections I had planned would work, and that in two weeks' time I would be safely home.

I took a taxi from the Woodlands MRT to the shuttle train to cross to Malaysia but there was lots of traffic (the taxi man was most apologetic), and the card I'd been given by the conference organisers to pay for any taxi ride with wouldn't work (it was only $8 so I didn't mind much). I then found, on arrival, that the train (which I hadn't been able to book) was sold out! What I hadn't realised was that the weekends are much busier than the weekdays, especially in June (school holidays) and on a Malaysian public holiday (as a friendly man I met in the bus queue told me).

So to Plan B – the first mishap on my journey requiring a last-minute change – a bus to Malaysia. I waited some time at the bus stop before another friendly man tipped me off to walk to customs and get the bus after that as they'd drop me there anyway to pass customs before I could continue to Malaysia! Customs was fine – I was the only European there it seemed amidst a sea of Malaysians but it was very, very busy and the bus queue took nearly an hour. There were queues of blue, smoke-belching Malaysian coaches crowding the road (which blocked the route so the scheduled busses couldn't get through, as everything had to come through a narrow passage under the customs building, enclosed and crowded with people and not very pleasant) and some 'causeway express' busses seemed to be coming more often than the 170 I was waiting for in a specific queue. A few of these came and went before I'd got far enough forward in the queue to board.

But I got there in the end, after an experience quite unlike anything I've seen in Britain. We crossed the causeway to Malaysia quickly and I was in good time for the 10:00 train from Johar Bahru to Gemas to begin a trek across Asia. JB station was posh, and I had to go through customs again to get to it – and there was, pleasingly, no electronic information (screens or announcements), just ticket-checking staff to ask which platform to go to. I loved that train! It wound slowly along a single track through amazing countryside like nothing I'd experienced before, and I used my seat little as the doors were wide open: too good an opportunity to miss to stand by said doors, enjoying the sights and smells of the passing countryside.

The train squealed as we rumbled along a single, rusty track, the old wooden sleepers still holding up the shrieking steel. The sun baked down from overhead, and I looked through the wide-open door – left that way to save the effort of having to close it, it seems – through large palm plantations, loosely interspersed with patches of jungle and the odd broken-down building: a cottage without its roof, a rusty tin shack. The doors on the train had signs warning of a hefty penalty for opening the doors while it was moving, but the guard didn't seem to care that they were open, or to bother shutting any of them – as it should be, I think, on the truly slow train going at such a speed that one could jump off at any time and probably not get hurt. It would be forbidden in my own, health-and-safety and protocol-obsessed fast-paced country, of course, where the Great Western Railway throws a fit if one but dares to open the window a notch and is doing its best to do away with opening widows altogether.

The palm is grown in long, shady avenues, sometimes with ditches dug for irrigation, sometimes the trees are tall, harvested over many years with trunks not topped by high-up leaves, sometimes they are short and squat. Occasionally the sight of tree-topped hills, green or grey depending on the distance, appears. And now and again more of the shabby buildings, wood or painted concrete, surround us in their numerous pretty shades, and we arrive at a dusty platform in a village or town. There, aerials teeter up into the air and sometimes shiny cars wait in lines on busy roads or at crossroads, seeming so out of place amidst the rustic carts and houses. Often there are motorbikes too. The stations are crumbling, with worn-out seats and aging loudspeakers whose sound, I presume, must be quite as ear-splitting as the loud, crackly announcements on the train's own tannoy. One has a sign advertising KTM the railway company, with the tagline 'ontime everytime [sic]'. One station, though, is decorated with pretty flowering bushes, pink. Sometimes we are above the palms, which form then a green mass; other times beneath them, when the corridors of dappled sun and brown discarded branches are visible. Sometimes a dirt track disappears amidst them; often they are close enough to touch – and certainly to smell, though usually the aroma of plant is displaced by that of dung.

At Gemas I bought some fruit for lunch, looked around the old, dishevelled, authentic town and caught an electric (alas) train to Kuala Lumpur. I was disappointed to find a nasty modern 'train' show up, on which the air conditioning was so cold that it made one shiver, and where there was no recourse to outside air, the doors and windows being sealed shut. Onboard there were television screens with frequent adverts being shown, and a quite hilarious introductory message played to introduce new passengers to the train at every stop, talking about the locations of the toilets as if it was a glamourous topic above cheesy music!

This journey was a somewhat different experience. Although the landscape outside was similar to before – perhaps with a greater variety of trees – we were now on a double-track flanked by posts holding electric cables and fencing that kept the vegetation decidedly away from the train. This was a modern, high-speed electric service, with doors that electronically closed and no escape from the air conditioning that made it feel little warmer than Britain on a cloudy day. Speakers played that nauseating music while automatic voices in Malay and English described the features of the train. There were visual screens that showed both the train's destination and adverts for 'magic flour' that could be used to make instant cakes and other such disgusting products. Meanwhile, the sunny morning had relapsed outside into a somewhat cloudy afternoon, There were sometimes goats grazing in the grass beside the track, and cattle grazing beneath the trees. Sometimes, the speakers would play more music and an animation wishing 'Ramadan Kareem' would show, this being that month in the Islamic calendar, before more adverts for 'freezy layer cake' et cetera. My eyes were more often pointed outside. 45 minutes in were revealed rolling tree-clad hills, hazy in the fog and looking beautiful as the mist rose above them in wispy clouds.

It had been sunny, but rain came in and it was seemingly impossible to get anywhere on foot from Kuala Lumpur station, so I got a taxi to the hotel where I'd already reserved a room. One pays the taxi in advance here, which I like. KL is full of busy, fume-spewing traffic with few crossings. The hotel is a big, posh tower, though only MR 139 (£25) I'd paid in advance. Lots of stairs to floor 15 (I hate using lifts!). I went out to explore, saw the busy bustle begin as evening came on and smelt some foul things (exhaust fumes and meat being sold or eaten on the streets). Chinatown was full of tat and nasty meaty food, but I eventually found a delicious meal at a vegetarian Indian restaurant, worth MR 30 (only £5). KL isn't the most pretty place, but was nonetheless a great experience.

## Day 2: Kuala Lumpur to Thailand
*Sunday 18th June*

*Padang Besar is a small town on the Thai-Malaysia border*

I had a good night's sleep, and walked back down the 15 flights to check out of the hotel, and back up to floor 6 for breakfast. You could have breakfast cereal – the first I've seen since arriving in Asia on Monday – and some fruit. There were also many strange things I didn't care to eat. It didn't take long, then I walked the short way to the monorail station and bought a token to KL Sentral. The trains are only two coaches here, leave approximately every 8 minutes and are sometimes somewhat slanted, it seems, when moving – the city's system is quite new and basic, not heavily used (indeed I hardly saw anyone else when using it). There are no monorail information screens, but there are screens in the sleek KL Sentral, a horrible station with a big shopping centre attached. I could have used the monorail to travel from the station to the hotel yesterday, which would have been cheaper than the taxi too (neither was expensive, but the monorail was very cheap indeed), but I'd have had no idea which line to use and where to get off for my hotel, whereas the central railway station is quite straightforward to find as all routes lead there.

The 8:00 from KL Sentral was another electric train with frigid air conditioning. I more liked the look of KL Historic station, which we stopped at – but KL is so hard to navigate on foot I'd not have found it had I wanted to use it (the historic station is not, alas, not easy to reach by monorail; it's a colonial-era design I believe but seems to have been abandoned recently in favour of the new monstrosity). Since it was another snazzy new train I stood by the doors where it was slightly warmer than in the heart of the air-conditioned carriages, for some of the journey. Outside were stretches of fantastic jungle-covered hills, with soft cushions of cloud, low atop the trees. Sometimes we moved into flatter, more open lands and sometimes through dirty cities, and the rain fell very heavily for a time. Approaching Thailand, the landscape became even more beautiful, if only because it was less hazy, when outcrops of rock like harder pillows sat cloaked in lush forest. Again, apart from these there was a mixture of jungle, plantation and habitation. After five hours we pulled into Padang Besar, just after noon Thai time, where is a large Malaysian KTM station, reasonably new and neat. At last I escaped the cheesy music and announcements, and stepped out into the hot sun.

Padang Besar was a lovely place to stay for a few hours on the way into Thailand. First, I found my way to the Malaysian checkpoint, then walked the short way to Thailand despite offers for transport – everyone here find it very strange to walk; it's 'too hot'. At customs, a man pulled me up out of the queue because I am European, and got me to fill in a form. When I said I had no address in Thailand as I'm just passing through, he said I had to have one or else I 'can't come in' – and told me to put down a hotel in Bangkok I was 'staying at'. I got the hint and tried 'Hotel Bangkok'. 'There is no hotel Bangkok', he said, 'try again.' So, I instead had to invent 'Hotel International Bangkok'. With this, he was pleased, returned my passport having stamped it and let me go.

A very friendly man on a motorcycle persuaded me to hop on to take me to the Thai railway station – so, I tried it, for the experience and because this time I didn't know where to go! He raced me through the streets, which are light on traffic, and tried to charge me 50 Thai Baht (not very much) but I had it seemed only 500 or 1000 notes that neither he nor anybody else would accept – though he did motor off with 1500 to see if he could change them. He came back and returned them, and I paid him in Malaysian Ringgit instead, with a tip! Everything is so cheap here I don't need the big notes. I walked into the main town (my train not being until 5) to explore, and the security guard at the 11-7 corner shop supermarket in these parts took me on his bike to where they'd change Ringgits to Baht – but even there they'd not take what I thought was a 500 Baht note. Of course, it later turned out I'd not been trying to exchange Baht at all, but Russian roubles!

I converted my Ringgits and spent the afternoon walking about. I eventually found some vegetarian food (nearly all has meat in it), getting a sweet omelette from one of the many street stalls. I ate lunch about 4, very hungry, sitting overlooking the main street. I got what I thought was vegetable noodles too, but it turned out it contained tiny bits of something that could conceivably be meat, so I had to throw that away. It isn't easy to know what you're getting here, when you don't speak the language.

Back at the station, by now very hot, I walked to the adjoining park but was warned by people manning the station quite vociferously not to be too long, as there were only '2 minutes' (they meant '20') left. One can't imagine such active interest at a station in England! There had also been a debacle about the website I'd bought my tickets from, '12go.asia', telling me to collect my train tickets on the Thai side, when actually they were at the Malaysian station. The nice man at the ticket office sent for them, and they were eventually delivered by motorbike (a train from the Malay side was supposed to bring them first, but apparently forgot). I got them in the end, and the five o' clock came roaring in on time.

The Thai station at Padang Besar is quite different from the Malaysian, and the train service delightfully more rustic. The station is a couple of miles from the border checkpoint, which is at the Malaysian one, and looks very new and clean, but not nastily glitzy and westernised like the new Malaysian ones: it is old-fashioned and distinctly Thai, of wood and white-washed walls. It is a single platform on a single line with a handful of trains per day, but has a ticket office where the staff are very friendly. I also saw some lizards at the station, and tried to find both stamps and a working telephone in vain (all were disconnected) to contact my dad on Father's Day – I wrote him a postcard instead.

I should like to be able to speak Thai, as hardly anyone speaks English in Thailand, in contrast to Malaysia where many do. On the train a man came and sat next to me and played English phrases on his telephone, but the Thai is so different I couldn't remember it easily. I rejected the offer of a (meat) meal on the train and ate my supplies from Padang Besar; also time to read and look out the window – but soon all was dark. A shame; the scenery may have been beautiful. Still, I must reach Bangkok somehow! The sunset is so sudden here. A lot of walking about in the hot sun this afternoon made up for enforced enclosure this morning and tonight!

The train from Padang besar to Bangkok was a rustic diesel with an open carriage where people could stand clutching ropes, an all-seated carriage and a sleeper carriage, with lower seats that transform into

19

beds and an upper berth above each set – my carriage. There was, alas, air-conditioning but not nearly so frigid as in Malaysia, the carriage wasn't crowded (I had it to myself at first) and it was very comfortable, looking out at a landscape of trees and rustic towns. We moved quite slowly in parts; the train wasn't either new or especially old. The first stop was brief, the second longer, at a larger station where women boarded attempting to sell chicken meat and fruit – I bought some pineapple – and we waited about 45 minutes. The engine was taken from the front and moved to the back, but though we briefly shunted the opposite way, alongside a broken down wreck of a train and piles of disused rotting wooden sleepers, we soon continued in the direction we had begun in. Some children, playing by the tracks, kicked a ball against the train window as we passed. I saw some cattle fighting in a clearing and pools, streams, trees and rough buildings, but soon the night fell.

## Day 3: Bangkok
### *Monday 19th June*

*A rustic scene approaching Bangkok*

I slept in an upper berth; originally there was nobody beneath me but the carriage, already getting fuller, entirely filled up overnight. Every berth has a thin foam mattress, pillow, thin sheet and blue curtain; the carriage lights were still visible in the upper berths but I managed to sleep despite the light, waking now and again. In the morning, I rose before 6 local time – just before sunrise – and found some spare seats at the end of the carriage where, an added bonus, the air conditioning had an especially small effect because of ventilation ducts in the automatic doors (they'd been taped over but some of the tape had come off!). Everyone else seemed to stay asleep for some hours. The view outside was beautiful pasture, jungle with muddy-banked streams, more pillow hills, shanty towns of cobbled-together huts and grazing beasts, coconut shapes hanging from trees in webby forms. I now saw that the carriage was made by Daewoo in Korea in 1996; it had lasted 21 years well.

At one point we stopped at a small station and somebody got on to walk the carriages selling more wares. He left the outer door open, so for some 20 minutes I could stand looking out at fields, paddies, people and jungle as we passed, the door catching on vegetation where the track was single and narrow – what a true joy! I now saw at last the explanation for last night's shenanigans with the engine. We had been shunted onto the back of another train, and I was now at the rear of some dozen carriages. It looked beautiful, curving its way through the countryside, its paint dirty and flaky white and dark red. That time with the door left open made my day, looking out and breathing the fresh air! I took many pictures.

We stopped a few times before pulling slowly through the dirty outskirts of Bangkok. I saw a dog walking on another track at one stage. Indeed, I saw some rather dirty slums, and people and other animals living right up to the rails. That was a very stark contrast to other parts of Bangkok I'd see later. Monday Morning Prayer's emphasis on Creation seemed especially wonderful, as I am now indeed on the other side of the Earth. We got to Bangkok a little late – soon after 10 – and it seemed a brilliant station, rather old-fashioned as I like. In all stations there is a picture – almost a shrine – to some leader in Thailand; Bangkok's Hua Lumpur station also has a pleasing grand façade.

The city itself is hard to navigate, as I found when I set out for a walk. I purposed to explore, but also to find an internet cafe to at last email home – I didn't know whether they got my telephone message from Singapore or not. I couldn't find one, and got very hot and sweaty. My shirt by tonight was now a filthy rag. In Bangkok there is lots and lots of traffic and one takes one's life in one's hands crossing roads – rarely are there pedestrian lights. I bought a big bottle of water, and, only finding internet gaming rooms, decided to try out the metro. By then I had seen many more old-fashioned streets, where people sold their wares. That was the best part.

I didn't like the metro; it was very new and shiny, clinical even, full of people weary shiny modern clothes and using smart 'phones. Nearly everyone on Singapore's metro was using those too; I don't see what everyone sees in them. I got off (it's only a single line here) at 'Thailand Cultural Centre', which proved to be nothing but a shopping mall and another busy road. I did find a Post Office and sent dad his postcard for Father's Day; the woman who served me had me write over the address in pen as I'd used pencil. Then I returned to the metro and went to the 'convention centre'. In both places were big, shiny, boring modern buildings – not the real Bangkok. That stop was half way to Hua Lumpur and I walked the rest, passing through a beautiful park. I was hungry by then (it was mid-afternoon) and went in search of vegetarian food, which I found after 3 at a sweet little café where a kindly woman made me 'morning glory' – a green leaf – fried with spices and rice – delicious!

Before that I'd seen a beautiful 'wat' – a sort of Temple area I think – and a woman had asked me lots of questions about where I was going. She wanted me to have my shirt sleeves cut off because of the heat! Opposite the station – where I'd begun – I found the internet café I'd sought, and spend 30 Baht (not much) on 45 minutes emailing home and checking some of the 100-odd emails that had accumulated since I left Britain.

I went to the station to read in the very large waiting area packed with people, then went to another place that served vegetables and rice for my evening meal, another 50 Baht. At the station, the 20:00 awaited on Platform 3; they'd put me in a women's-only carriage so I had to go and get the ticket swapped! Alas, it was a much newer version of yesterday's train, air-conditioned and with smarter, red berths. The staff on the train seemed friendly. It was dark and had begun raining heavily when we left. I had a slight headache from all that sun and was quite tired.

## Day 4: Thailand to Laos
### *Tuesday 20th June*

*You can get anywhere from Vientiane*

I spent most of the journey from Bangkok to Nong Khai on the Thai border again on the upper berth; it may have been a sleeker, very new train with smart furnishings but the ride was not much smoother, and alas it was no longer possible to escape the horrible air conditioning. Nobody got on trying to sell any wares; instead a refreshments trolley was sent through this morning. I preferred the older, more authentic train. It was of course already dark and raining when we set off, but today I arose about 4:30 local time (5:30 in the Malaysia time I've been used to) and it was light enough to see trees, fields and paddies pass, and the odd neat rural station. The part of Thailand approaching Laos is very flat. I do miss my early morning walks, being on these trains! I read for a little while, and we arrived a little late at Nong Khai, the Thai side of the border. Another beautiful, old station.

There isn't much at Nong Khai station; I was misled at first in walking out of the station, but soon realised (the station is in the middle of nowhere) that I had to go back inside to go any further. From there, one can buy a ticket for a shuttle train to Thenalang, just over the Laos border, and a 'minivan' on to Vientiane, the capital of Laos, not far away. The shuttle is a wonderful, battered old machine, not very big, and leaves at about 7:30. It takes you over the river; there are checkpoints on the platforms at either end. I boarded when the engine had revved up for a while – a lovely old banger of a two-carriage train! Someone was filling it up with water from a hose.

We crossed a wide river, a small group of passengers: there were some German women, an English young man and an American woman backpacking, and an older English man with a Thai woman – one occasionally sees such couples. Arriving in Laos requires one to pay US $36 for a short-stay visa; at Thenalang we had to fill in visa application forms (again I had to invent a hotel, now in Laos) but they didn't pay much attention, eager for our US dollars, and gave us the visas. I even filled my form in in pencil! The minivan to Vientiane from the tiny station was included with the shuttle ticket; it was quite a long way – too far to walk – and they set us down at the central bus station. It was by then nearly 9 in the morning.

Alas, I was tricked by a 'put-put' driver into being driven by him, with two monks, into the city centre. He said it was far away but it turned out to be easy walking distance, and it cost me 50 000 Laos kip, which is a lot – 200 Thai baht or nearly £5, a standard fare it seems. I hadn't brought any kip so had to exchange some Baht; I did so several times in all today, having a few things to buy.

I spent this morning exploring the city; it's a fantastic place, with many beautiful Wats – temples – and a wonderful central monument that is hundreds of years old. It has a rather French feel (Laos was French once, after all) with many restaurants and very few street stalls, a contrast with Thailand. Everywhere I walked I was offered a put-put again and again, the locals evidently eager to have the custom of a foreign traveller. The Mekong river is set back from the town by a wide green bank, and is very pretty. I read in a park – where women offered me manicures (which I did not take up) – and had lunch in a café where I met a socialist American, whom I enjoyed discussing politics and climate change with. As far as I can tell, socialists are not that common in America – after all, he isn't in America any more, and I suspect there's a reason for that. My vegetable rice was 15 000 Kip (about £1.30).

I bought a salad baguette to eat while travelling this evening (the French influence again – I've not seen much of that sort of thing hereabouts) from a sweet old lady, and realising I'd left my writing pencil on the floor where I'd dropped it by the (really rather rustic) toilet block I had to return to get it, bringing me back to an ethical crafts shop I'd earlier seen a bracelet in that I thought of buying for someone. That was a sure sign I should swap one of my remaining unused US dollars for Kips so as to have enough to buy it after all.

I returned on foot to the central bus station, which was chaotic, with busses and people all over the place, but aided by several kindly people I found the right place to wait and caught a busy bus to the southern bus station, where my overnight bus to Hanoi was to depart from. The journey through Vientiane offered further possibility of seeing the beautiful buildings and avenues of the city, many of them a splendid white. I got to the southern bus station early, and eventually found the right place to redeem my reservation for a ticket on the bus, but they wouldn't let us board until 6 (the scheduled departure time) so I had to wait for a long time amidst all the pollution and heat.

As the journey at last began (we seemed to wait around for quite a while before the family running the bus were ready to go) I was unable to read because the light was too low, so listened to 'The Hitchhiker's Guide to the Galaxy', of all things, on the MP3 Player I'd brought to serve as an alarm clock (at which function it had failed). Thankfully the places I visited weren't quite as wacky as that!

At about 6pm every day (the actual timing is quite relaxed while the bus company see whether they can fill the last spaces on the bus) the sleeper bus departs from Vientiane in Laos to Hanoi in Vietnam. There are several other such busses each evening run by rival companies, and I witnessed a competition between those young men organising my bus in their bright green T-shirts and another group – in pale orange – running another bus, trying to get a man to use their service. My ticket being booked online in advance, I didn't have to choose which bus to ride.

The sleeper bus, as one sees when they eventually let you in, contains three rows of seats front-to-back, each with a lower and upper berth and corridors between the rows. The bus was mostly filled, and I was on the lower berth by the right-hand window. Since we were still not far from the equator it was soon dark, encouraging an early night, but we stopped at about 10:30 – seemingly at the same place that other busses also stopped – at a large warehouse-like building with no front side (as is common hereabouts). Here, some people bought food from a servery – at such a late hour! A television was on, playing a Vietnamese music channel with some quite groan-worthy visual accompaniment to the music. As we went off again into the night, I fell asleep.

*A Wat is a common sight in Laos*

# Day 5: Vietnam
*Wednesday 21st June*

*Motorbikes choke even the more old-fashioned parts of Hanoi*

In the morning it became clear why there had been no rush leaving Vientiane. We had stopped at some point during the night at the border, as had the other busses queueing mostly behind us, and couldn't cross until it opened for the day. I woke at 5:45, and it turned out the bus drivers were asleep, having left the bus door open so that we could go out to stretch our legs (I did so) or buy some food. Alas, being so high in the mountains it was heavily raining, making it less pleasant outside.

I must confess that today was not so enjoyable as those of late, as much of it was spent sitting on a bus and I hate sitting down for long periods! It seemed a long time before the checkpoint opened, about 7, and there was then a lot of waiting around – giving in passports to get them checked and stamped first in Laos then in Vietnam. I stood for a while in the little shack serving food until we were allowed to present our passports in the chaotic Laos departures office, and were let through to board the bus again. We then drove a short way to the Vietnamese checkpoint to go through the process again, getting what shelter we could from the rain; here they charged US $1 for the stamp on each passport. It was a good thing I had a dollar left! A young man and woman from Britain didn't have enough Laos kip or Vietnamese dong to use instead, so I gave them 10 000 kip I had spare; that's less than £1, the kip is so weak. The dong is even weaker, and just as Laos seemed poorer than Thailand seemed poorer than Malaysia seemed poorer than Singapore, so in material terms Vietnam made Laos look rich!

The bus had to be searched again before we could board and continue. At least the views were spectacular in the forested mountains entering Vietnam, little diminished by the rain. The Vietnamese side of the checkpoint was dilapidated, with people huddled into small spaces under corrugated iron roofs to keep off the rain, but Vietnam appeared to be beautifully rustic. Having begun in the majestic mountains we soon descended into the plain, where there were many farms. There were people working the fields with straw hats, western clothes, and with sparse animals of various kinds helping them farm in a good old-fashioned way.

There were hammer-and-sickle signs in red in the villages and towns we passed, which always seemed to be stretched out along the road. Despite these shows of communism, I saw many signs of capitalist control here.

At about 11 o' clock we stopped for 45 minutes or more at another of those food depots, and while others ate (I had bought some bread in Vientiane) I went for a pleasant walk through some streets and fields nearby, until it started raining again. There were views to take photographs of to show everyone at home. One of my fellow passengers was saying how he too was going to Nanning, where I am to stop off on my way from Hanoi to Beijing, but he is getting a bus tomorrow, I a train tonight. He was most interesting to talk with. There was only a brief petrol stop after that, around 2, when I was told off for not wearing shoes when I stepped off briefly (they have us remove shoes on the bus to keep it clean, of course, but I don't like wearing shoes anyway) but I did wipe my feet clean on re-embarking!

We were supposed to reach Hanoi no later than 15.30, but as time went on there were still signs saying there was over 100 km to go. We didn't go especially slowly and I don't know why it took longer than planned; perhaps it was the checkpoint this morning? About 100 km from Hanoi we reached an expressway that allowed us to increase our speed somewhat, but we were still nearly two hours late in arriving. It was terrible not being able to walk for so long. I passed the time learning some Chinese in a phrase book I bought yesterday from an international language bookshop, and listening to the end of 'The Hitchhiker's Guide to the Galaxy' to ease the tedium. More signs and huge advertisement boards passed by. Though the hills and fields were pleasant, none of the settlements we passed seemed especially interesting, and I was very glad to get off the bus soon after 5, albeit into the horribly polluted Vietnamese capital.

When we eventually arrived, I left the bus as quickly as I could and set off walking north towards the railway station, having seen the rough whereabouts of it in relation to the bus station on a nearby map. However, I didn't realise quite how big Hanoi is – what the scale of the map was – and the railway station was on the opposite side of the city (quite inconveniently). After an hour and a half walking along the main road and exploring more scenic back-streets where I could, I was still, it later turned out, much less than half way there.

Hanoi is a terribly polluted city, with swarms of motorbikes everywhere – both on the main road (more like a motorway but with buildings on either side) and throughout all the smaller streets, belching out a lot of noise and smoke. These were the main cause of the poor air quality, there being very few cars. A good government would ban them and replace them with bicycles (of which there are still a few surviving it seems); they are a real menace on every street. The air was barely breathable, and I feel very sorry for the inhabitants.

I met some people at a bus stop to ask directions, and a young lady who knew some English helped me (I have no Vietnamese) and even walked me to the correct bus stop ( a little way away) and boarded the No.3 bus with me, most kindly! I do meet such generous people on my travels here, and it is just as well because something as obvious as a station is very difficult to find, with no signage or information about it anywhere. The bus took half an hour to get there, through endless busy streets and over a river. When in the right vicinity, I set about trying to find somewhere to get some nutritious vegetarian food, eventually buying rice and vegetables near the station from a friendly lady in her small eatery.

Overall, Hanoi was not a pleasant place, despite many of the people I met there being lovely: very polluted air, very difficult to navigate through, full of traffic and shops of various kinds. There was very little English signage – not that that counts against the place, after all why should they put up signs in English? – compared to other South-east Asian cities I've seen. It seemed endless, and it transpired that the railway station was right in the north-east corner. It seemed a tiny station indeed, for such a large city, tucked away behind a residential district with a very small waiting room. I later found that it was separate to the main railway station, which uses a different gauge of track – through-trains to China on Standard Gauge only departed from here. There were about two dozen people in it, and a single platform, as far as I could see.

A lady sent on behalf of Baolau (the company from whom I'd ordered my ticket online) met me there 45 minutes before the train to give me my ticket; she could guess it was me presumably because I was the only westerner amidst Chinese and Vietnamese faces. She said, however, that they'd been unable to obtain the ticket for the second half of the journey I'd booked with them, from Nanning to Beijing, and that I'd have to buy it myself at Nanning. I had to hope that there were some available! She also frightened me by saying that food and drink wouldn't be allowed across the border, when I'd just bought a pineapple and a 1.5 litre bottle of water!

She saw me safely onto the train, and we left on time at 21:20 with Chinese efficiency. It was a lovely train, with carpeted corridor on one side and compartments on the other, plus an attendant for each carriage. There is space to stand and look out in the corridor. I was in a lower berth – No. 17 – in a compartment shared with three others. We could switch off the light this time, making for a good sleep, though it was interrupted twice by immigration checks.

At 1 in the morning we arrived at the Vietnam border and had to queue to have our passports stamped. The train waited some time there at Dong Dong, then we moved on and at 2:30 arrived at the first Chinese station, where I had to fill in an arrival form. Again we queued and they scanned our baggage, but they didn't search our luggage or confiscate foodstuffs. A sign reassured us that they were trying to keep the experience as friendly as possible, and we could rate the experience at the end on a computer touch-screen. I gave my passport policeman top marks.

It was a good night, really, on that train – the motion soon sends one back to sleep – but it was on waking in the morning that I had the real treat of this journey. Bleary-eyed, I looked out on beautiful cliffs on the scattered hillocks, like those seen in Thailand but more in number, mysterious in a slight mist that made the bare rocky parts look like rags tied on hanging lines atop the vegetation. There was farmland too, and we passed through a city's outskirts, with tower-blocks visible in the hazy distance, but mostly all was rock and forest and astounding to behold – South China!

These hills held an aura of adventure indeed, with space to stand or sit and watch the view amply afforded by my train: it felt most luxurious compared to the coach. But for some reason every few seconds or so the train horn sounds (it really does sound like a hoarse horn), perhaps because of the mist. We arrived in Nanning soon after 10 to a warm, humid atmosphere.

*Arriving into China*

# Day 6: Nanning
*Thursday 22nd June*

*The hills of South China provide a beautiful welcome*

Of all the places I'd been on this trip, the south of China must be the most astoundingly beautiful. Awaking this morning at around 6 I was greeted by an immensely pleasing sight: picturesque tree-clad hills, now on this side now on that. There is some development here – notably the big city of Nanning where I spent most of the day – but largely it is green, beautiful, life-filled countryside. The milky sky above, casting a soft light, made it seem all the more wonderful.

I arrived at Nanning at about 10:10 and had been scheduled on my original itinerary to leave almost straight away at about 11 on another train, to Beijing.

However, the woman who gave me my ticket from the company I'd booked it with at Hanoi told me a schedule change meant that they couldn't book the second leg of the journey, and would refund me – I would have to obtain the Nanning to Beijing ticket myself.

I found my way down to the ticket office as quickly as I could (Nanning station is large and difficult to navigate, and the entrance is separate to the exit) and an English-speaking assistant helped me buy a ticket for over 400 yuan (the going rate, but nearly all my Chinese cash!) Alas, all the trains this morning were sold out already so it had to be the 17:38 departure, in a 'hard berth' sleeper coach as planned. Instead of 10 o' clock tomorrow, I'll hence get to Beijing at 5 (it's about a 24 hour journey), so I was worried today because I'd need to get to my pickup-point for my ticket on the Trans-Siberian before their office closed for the weekend.

I wandered around Nanning for some time, and found it a not unpleasant place, albeit with too many shops in vast underground corridors (I got lost looking for the metro down there, just as I had one day in Singapore). It struck me how very, very quiet it is in the streets (despite being busy), and how breathable the air is, compared to Hanoi – then I realised that all the motorbikes I saw here, indeed every without exception, were electric, not petrol. What a difference that makes: a brilliant idea! China gives me much more hope than Vietnam, in this respect.

I spent some hours searching for either a telephone or – very importantly – an internet café. Yes, I used one only a few days ago, but now I knew that I was going to be late to Beijing I needed to get in touch with the Trans-Siberian ticket company, or at least get in touch with home for a message to be sent on. It's not so easy as it used to be to find these, as so many people have internet-connected mobile 'phones nowadays, and you might be tempted to argue that I too ought to have had a mobile 'phone – except that it all worked out well without one anyway.

I went into one tower-block of shops up to the second floor in search of somewhere I could access the internet without success, and when I asked a motorbike driver outside where one might be, he wanted paying to show me! The trouble is that though I was always with my phrasebook in hand today, trying to learn basic Chinese (I now know the symbol for the first syllable of 'internet café' very well, having sought for it desperately on every sign I see), my unpractised pronunciation is very poor and it's hard to get things across. In Chinese, pronouncing the same sound differently gives it a different meaning. On the streets of a typical Chinese city, barely anyone speaks any English – which is a good thing I think.

Eventually somebody else pointed me the right way and I found myself in a dark room full of computers on which dozens of young men were playing computer games. The 'café' organisers were most helpful, enabling me to access a Virtual Private Network so that I could get round the Great Firewall of China and access Google (which is blocked officially) to log onto email. I found the 'phone number to call for the Trans-Siberian office but then faced the problem of there being no public callboxes in Nanning! At least I could get a message home. Somebody offered me his mobile to use but I dialled the number wrong I think (including the +86 access code for China at the beginning) – it obviously wasn't meant to be that I get in touch with them!

I managed to buy some lunch of rice, vegetables and tofu from somewhere I managed to get the concept of vegetarianism over to, eventually. A rather tiring day! I wended my way around the station at length, and of course had to be scanned on the way in, as they do in China. They made me drink some of my water to prove what it was! You aren't allowed onto a platform until your train arrives, and each train has a designated waiting room, where you literally wait until you are fetched. This was crowded. We were held like sheep in a pen until the departure time approached, then herded down to the platform.

The train left bang on time, and I found myself in a six-sleeper 'hard' compartment. The sunset mountain views were most spectacular. There were two very friendly Chinese men in the compartment with me whom I tried to speak a little with. They were as communicative as they possibly could be, given that they spoke not a word of English and I barely a word of Chinese! In this type of train there is no carpet in the corridor, but they do have fold-down seats that people from upper berths can sit on and look at the view. A woman pushes a trolley through from time to time, sometimes with meals, sometimes with buckets of fruit (some of which had been stored under our bunks and retrieved) or other like things.

As on many Asian trains, I've found, the toilets were in the form of holes in the floor, with no paper or soap (you are to bring your own) – though I did find a proper toilet in the disabled carriage when pacing the train for exercise. They're not especially clean either. When the train stopped at stations some of us got out to stretch our legs, but there were few such stops on the high-speed 23.5-hour journey to Beijing. I was glad to not be on one of the super-fast 13.5 hour bullets to Beijing instead, as I suspect those would be horribly modern trains that would make me feel ill. Here, the air conditioning was pleasantly weak, so it didn't feel like sitting in a refrigerator, the beds were perfectly comfortable (I had a good night's sleep) and there was space to stand (and even smoke for those so inclined!) at the ends of the carriages. I was impressed.

# Day 7: To Beijing
*Friday 23rd June*

*A mixture of traditional and modern in China's capital*

I awoke to find a beautiful landscape outside the train, with more of the forests and hills of south China. Again I was to be travelling all day, but unlike my day on the bus on Wednesday at least I would have the train carriage to walk around in, not confined to one place!

We were due to be on the train until 17.03 according to the schedule (not likely to be far wrong in China), which meant a lot of time for reading and – at last – for writing other things than just this journal, which I have not been inclined to do on other journeys when it has been only early or late in the day that I've had a quiet place to think (the bus was certainly not conducive to this!); this train afforded just such an opportunity.

I didn't have much with me for breakfast and lunch, but made the most of what I had (I did not trust to buy any on-train meals, as I suspect they all contain meat and the packaging is very excessive). I still had some oat biscuits given me on the Malaysian train when they handed out free goodie-bags to everyone, a peach, the end of my bread from Laos and three small tomatoes. It was sufficient. They only provide boiling water on the train (habitual tea-drinkers would be well-supplied) so alas I had to be a bit wasteful in bottling some and waiting for it to cool down before drinking it.

We stopped at three places during waking hours, at about 9.30, 11.08 and 14.33, on time, giving a chance to briefly go outside. The day passed neither too slowly nor too quickly for my taste, and at 17.06 (shockingly late!) we arrived at Beijing East. I don't think three minutes' delay is too bad for such a long journey.

I now needed to get my Trans-Siberian ticket with which I could continue my journey to Europe, before the office closed at 6. I raced to the metro but you had to join a long queue to have your things scanned by security. The station had been modified with temporary barriers, implying that this was a new thing. It was quite excruciating after this trying to buy a metro ticket from a machine that was very fussy with notes, then waiting to get to Chang Wen Men station. A rather hyperactive teenager on the train was saying things to me because I'm English that I couldn't understand!

When I finally arrived at the correct metro station, it proved very difficult to find 'Beijing Business World' (it didn't have a sign outside the building or anything of that sort) and by the time I got there it was too late. Fortunately, however, they had left for me a telephone number to ring – a great relief, and I hoped I could telephone from my hotel.

Finding the hotel wasn't all that easy, either. I somehow set off walking in the wrong direction, and had to get the metro again to put me back in the right area. However, when I emerged from the station it was raining extremely heavily and dark. I got soaked – despite my small fold-up umbrella – by the time I found where roughly to go, then as the rain eased a young woman approached me and said she'd walk with me to give me directions, which was most kind and very helpful. I found the hotel at last amidst a busy commercial district near the centre of the city, a not unpleasant location.

The hotel was decorated in a traditional Chinese style, but they insisted on me paying a deposit in cash of 200 yuan so I had to go and get more from a cash machine. They generously allowed me to use their 'phone to call the company with the Trans-Siberian ticket, and I could pick it up at another office tomorrow, which made me feel much better.

With that sorted, I could go out and explore a little of Beijing, and found straight away a charming old-fashioned street where I could buy some oily but at least vegetarian spring rolls to eat. I ate in the main street amidst so many modern buildings. A man happened to meet me as I was returning to the hotel and showed me some of his beautiful Chinese drawings. He said he was soon going to Birmingham University in the UK, and I agreed to buy a set to give to my dad, since I obviously missed Father's Day last Sunday and he works at that same university – call me gullible if you will, but they're nice pictures, and weren't all that expensive. They would be a happy memento, if I ever got home!

*Beijing is home to some fantastic architecture.*

# Day 8: In Beijing
*Saturday 24th June*

*Chairman Mao's mausoleum seemed strangely quiet.*

I liked Beijing very much, for all the rain and confusion I experienced last night. It was also very pleasant to sleep soundly and wake in a stationary room for the first time since I left Kuala Lumpur six days ago, and to have a shower again! I was able to go straight out after that for an early walk, as I like to do when not confined to a bus or a train, and went to visit Tiananmen Square, not very far away. It seemed amazing to be able to so casually go to such a place, which normally would seem to be on the other side of the world, and it is very beautiful. There weren't many people there so early in the morning; you had to go through security checks though.

I came back through a very elegant park, and Beijing certainly seemed somewhat less high-rise and much less polluted than many of the cities I've seen recently, which pleased me. There were lots of electric motorbikes and electric busses around. It was a good place to be on this special day – Midsummer's Day in the northern hemisphere, and St John the Baptist's Day which I do celebrate. It was much better weather today, too – rather hot, but with mixed sun and cloud so not too intense, and not raining.

I next had to venture back to Beijing Business World where this time, from an alternative office that opened on a Saturday, I was finally able to collect my precious Trans-Siberian ticket! That was a great relief; the Trans-Siberian runs only twice a week and anyway has to be booked in advance, so I'd have been very delayed without this. It was only on my way back to the hotel that I found somewhere to buy a little breakfast; a sweet seed bar and some Chinese fruit that I don't know the name of was the best I could do! Earlier, I had visited a tea shop and bought a very good Green Tea that went down very well. The tea-bag was strong enough to use again so I filled one of my empty water bottles with tea, having run out of drinking water, back at the hotel.

After checking out of the hotel, and waiting for them to check the room thoroughly before they'd give me back my deposit, I walked to the Forbidden City – a truly beautiful place. The forecourt was absolutely packed with people queueing up for tickets so instead of queueing and going into the main Palace Museum I bought a small guide-book that has photographs and explanations in it of the whole place. Just after that I was set upon by lots of young Chinese people wanting to take photographs of me because I am English – how curious! I suppose it is possible that they have never seen a European before, if they are visiting Beijing from elsewhere in China.

After that I went into the People's Culture Palace, also part of the Forbidden City but with barely any queue (and only 15 yuan to get in) – though visitors still had to go through security for this. It was amazing. I don't think I've ever seen a man-made construction more beautiful. There were many old shrine buildings, one of which contained huge 'peace bells', and a beautiful water garden. I took many photographs of the wonderful buildings and am very glad I went in; it was pleasant also to sit in the gardens for a time.

After that, it was back to Tiananmen Square – much busier by now – to get a closer look at some of the monuments there. Curiously, the only part of the square that was still completely empty was the area around Mao's Mausoleum, which appeared to be deserted. I resisted going in the railway museum (I didn't really have time) but bought a cheap lunch of spicy cucumber nearby which was very refreshing.

Thus the afternoon drifted by in sunny Beijing. I found an internet café near the centre to contact home, where I hear it's been as hot as it is here for a short time; today was a perfect 28 degrees here. I had my evening meal in a steamed bun restaurant that had a vegetarian option; it was a bit expensive for what it was, but it's authentically Chinese at least. I bought the famous 'Tales of a thousand and one  Nights' from an International Book Store – not a Chinese book by any means but it was going very cheaply and would serve me well through the travels ahead – then made the half an hour walk over to Beijing railway station.

It was hard to find the actual entrance, as there were long queues of people going through security checks and at first I mistook them for ticket queues. It was a very busy station to wait in, and though it was already dark outside I had a while to wait for the 23:00 departure. As before, you couldn't descend to the platforms until your train was called, so I found myself sitting (or standing) in a long corridor with various shops full of various tat along the walls. This time of night is late for me, so I was getting tired. It was very exciting, though, when at last the train was due – the famous Trans-Siberian Express! Clutching my precious ticket, I made my way with the others to the long train that looked like a series of tin cans in the gloomy light, and was directed along to the correct carriage where its attendant was waiting to check the ticket. So ended my brief exploration of China, which I would miss; and so began a whole new adventure: six days aboard the Trans-Siberian Express.

# Day 9: Aboard the Express
## *Sunday 25th June*

*The Trans-Siberian Express*

I had begun my journey through China in the south, watching the golden sunset on sparsely-populated mountains leaving Nanning, while my journey to Beijing brought me to the much more densely populated eastern plain where most Chinese live, though even here there were plenty of fields and trees quite like parts of the English countryside, albeit with fewer woods and more buildings interspersed. Some of the Chinese buildings (especially tower-blocks) look very run-down, and the general standard of building in China outside the city centres is more akin to that of Malaysia than that of Britain, say. I passed many coal-fired power stations belching smoke and steam into the atmosphere and many, many pylons – testament to China's recent fast-paced industrialisation.

Photographs cannot capture, nor the portraits of the pen, what beauty is to be seen aboard the famous Trans-Siberian train line right across Russia. I took the route from Beijing to Moscow via Manchuria (there is an alternative via Mongolia that takes a little longer), the full extent of the line, and today was my first spent entirely on that train. This first day was spent going north and slightly east out of China, where lush woods on hills, proudly painted red-and-white chimneys of power stations and cities of great towers – some shabby, some sleek – continued to mark the landscape, though the wonder of the southern forests had been somewhat left behind.

The prospect of the journey was exciting, though when faced with its reality I felt that this would be an experience better shared with others, a time to be together, rather than seen alone. I was alone in my compartment (which could sleep up to six people) and indeed the train was sparsely populated. Perhaps the journey is more popular in the eastwards direction, I wonder. There were quite a few Chinese in some parts of the train, but I suspected they might disembark before Russia.

When I awoke before six this morning, I went straight for a walk all along the train to both ends, exploring its entire length and getting a feel for it. My empty compartment was a good, quiet place for contemplation, and my points of concentrated contact with God in prayer at 8, 1 and 6 became important times around which each day could revolve. Sometimes I stood to read out in the corridor of a carriage or in the space between carriages, where the light came in through the windows in the doors; sometimes I sat to

51

write or read (my bed lifted to become a set of three seats). This morning I wrote a poem about my travels, and how I only regret not getting back quickly to see everyone at home, whom I now much miss.

The train stopped four times today in places where we could get out and stretch our legs – and enjoy the sunshine where the platform roof didn't block it! – for five to fifteen minutes. I needed some good brisk walks, but at the first stop the Chinese platform official blew his whistle at me as if I was committing some crime in simply walking down the platform (that's how strict it is at stations in China), and the Russian lady in charge of our carriage seemed to want me to stay near that. Really, it makes it feel as though we're prisoners on this train, being allowed out into the prison yard only on very strict conditions. I'm also not allowed to go, inside, to the back of the train, where I'd wanted to stand watching the rear view – another Russian carriage attendant soon fetched me back when I tried that!

I confess I didn't feel entirely comfortable with all this, and for the first time really missed home, but it wasn't all that bad. For breakfast I had some sort of fruit pastry I bought in Beijing, and while I was praying before lunch the Chinese couple in the next compartment came and gave me some spare packets of bread and biscuits of theirs, which is very kind and would come in very useful.

I finished the pastry for my lunch, and hence not having eaten much I was eager for an evening meal after our final brief stop-off at 6.35. However, the Chinese were currently running the restaurant car, and wouldn't except roubles – on a Russian train! I hadn't brought any spare yuan, expecting the roubles would be what I needed. The lady was quite emphatic in telling me to get out; they wouldn't serve me. I cobbled together whatever yuan I could find and went back; then she said they were closed and offered me a left-over meat dish, which of course I couldn't have. So, it was more fruit bread (of a different kind) for me, and a few nuts I managed to buy with roubles from the carriage attendant who offers a very limited at-seat service. Thus, I survived alright, but hungry and in want of some proper food. The views were at least delicious outside, and though it rained a little it was mostly hot and sunny, and hence warm in the train too.

## Day 10: Into Russia
*Monday 26th June*

*Old steam trains are kept as ornaments at Russian stations*

Another day aboard the Trans-Siberian Express! It was very hot everywhere we went today, in excess of 30 degrees I'm sure. The light lasts so long now that we are far up in the North, with sunset at nearly 9, that it proves quite a contrast from the equatorial regions I was in before. We were woken soon after 4 in Beijing time (the same as Singapore time) and, rather than having to go out, we were checked out of China by customs officials boarding the train. They took our passports and we were all left waiting for over an hour, hoping that they'd give them back!

During this time we were, gladly, allowed to leave the train so my early walk was up and down the platform, shouted at by Chinese officials if I dared stray beyond what they deemed to be a permissible zone. There were only a handful of passengers on the train by then, the Chinese carriage and dining car (along with its vociferous rouble-hating woman) having been detached and gone, but I met an Australian couple and some Chinese friends whom I spoke to again at various points during the day. There is also a Chinese girl eager to learn some English; she gave me an apple and I gave her some paper, and later she suggested teaching each other some pronunciation using my phrasebook, which was good. The syllables are pronounced quite differently to what the book implies!

On receiving our passports back we rolled on to Russia, where after a short time we stopped again. The Russian immigration officials are even stricter than the Chinese. A gang of them came aboard with sniffer dogs (looking for drugs I presume) which were quite gently dogs really but searched every nook and cranny. Because my passport is seven years old and I had shorter hair then, at 17, they took a long time deciding that it was really mine, getting me to stand up, sit down and pull different facial expressions in the compartment then in the corridor outside. Having consulted for a long time together the three of them eventually decided to let me through. I had already been through twelve immigration checks on this journey (entering and leaving each country), and nowhere had I had any problem with my passport photo until now. I think they flatter Russia to make out that people are more eager to fraudulently sneak their way in there than anywhere else.

When the officials left, we were free to roam the station and adjacent border town for over 4 hours. The town we were in was the poorest place I have been to in my travels, dusty streets with old-banger cars looking very run-down. It isn't much to look at, a jumble of shacks and tatty houses, and shops (which are difficult to tell from the houses) in marked contrast to the smart Chinese tower-blocks just a few miles away, which looked like classic Russian buildings in some cases with their great golden domes. No such structures in this poor part of Russia. Probably it gets very cold in winter; for us at mid-summertime it was boiling hot – as hot as the tropics, so it seemed – and we had actually moved further east to a BST +8 time-zone, one hour ahead of Singapore and Beijing, though I ignored this and kept running on the other time zone.

In all there is a six-hour stop at this Russian town, during which the gauge of the carriages is changed to fit the wide Russian tracks. It was interesting seeing an old Orthodox church and having a good walk; it was too hot to walk for all that time, though, and some from the train went to the airy station café to talk for a bit. I bought some fruit for supplies – and carrots for some proper vegetables at last – from a shop where a man was perplexed I didn't speak any Russian but pointed instead. I looked for a Russian phrasebook but could only find, after much searching, in one shop a

Russian-English dictionary that had no pronunciation guide at all.

In the sun on the platform I read a book that took me back to England through poetry. Meanwhile, they had widened the gauge and put on a new engine, and we could get going. After another half an hour we stopped again, and many, many Russians got aboard – I now share my compartment with one man. This afternoon I wrote a poem, an essay on South-East Asian development and some fiction. The man thought that I was a journalist! While many people were boarding and waving goodbye to their families at one station, the Russian national anthem was played through the station loudspeakers, making it really quite a dramatic affair. Perhaps they had not been west before, or would not be coming back for a long time.

The Chinese carriages having gone it became a proper Russian experience on board, with roubles accepted in a dining car selling quite costly (with hidden charges) but pleasant food, for example, although when I went there tonight they only had mushrooms, peas and potato suitable for vegetarians, apparently being low on stocks – so a good thing I bought that carrot! It took 40 minutes to prepare so must have been fresh; I read while I waited. No Russians came into the dining car at all, so it was very empty. It was good to eat with a lovely view, and I was grateful for a proper meal.

# Day 11: Lake Baikal
*Tuesday 27th June*

*Lake Baikal is beautiful from the train*

After travelling north and somewhat east out of Beijing, it was only yesterday evening that we began to move west, and we awoke this morning with the sun behind us. The railway line was then running through a landscape of great empty plains and hills – I know not whether so vast an area could have been logged by man, or is naturally bare – surrounding us majestically as we went, putting me in mind of moors at home. Their bald heads ringed lakes and occasional pools of human habitation – Eastern Siberia.

As we turned West, though, we began to enter more mixed lands with deep pockets of woods, where men herded cattle on horseback or cultivated crops in little postcard plots at the backs of huddled wooden houses. It was an idyllic and enchanting vista, albeit mixed in with the creaking metal of ugly Russian industry that reared its head here and there, bringing us back to the present age. The sight of the misty hills clad with trees was breath-taking.

Thus I continued my westwards journey on the Trans-Siberian Express, today experiencing perhaps the most amazing scenery of the whole trip. I switched to BST +6 on waking today, gaining an hour's sleep (which made up for the rather early rise on crossing the Chinese border the night before) and rising at 5.30 in this new time zone to pace the train for my early-morning walk. My Russian compartment companion seemed to sleep a lot; perhaps, I thought, he has little else to do and is in need of rest.

We had two long stops today, at 09.21 and 17.48 on the clock I'm running to, though the trains in Russia all use Moscow time which is BST+2 and is entirely inappropriate for this longitude! That gave me chance to stretch my legs with a good brisk walk on both occasions, exploring the quite large stations of Urlan-Ude and Irkutsk. One can get off to walk about at all station stops so long as they are longer than 2-3 minutes, and the Russians are much, much more relaxed than the Chinese about where you can go – you can even walk on the tracks if you want to risk it.

At Irkutsk the Australian couple left (I didn't see them), as did my compartment companion so this evening I had the compartment to myself again. I couldn't speak with him, of course, but he seemed friendly and asked 'Russia is OK or not OK?'. He wore a cross. We allowed some children (running about expending energy) to use our compartment during their hide-and-seek game; they were a jolly presence in the carriage!

Another brief stop we made was at a station that didn't even have platforms, only some gravel next to the railway lines. Parts of Russia are very rustic, and I like that. I spent the morning reading, writing letters to tell some old friends about my travels, and simply looking out at the view. At 5 BST I felt very drowsy – my body always wants to sleep then, and wake up when I usually would at home at 5.45! There seemed a long time between stops today and I felt especially tired this afternoon – probably not helped by a nutritionally deficient diet of Russian bread, cucumber and apple. Hence I sat for some time writing about this railway and how transformative it must have been, the inspiring landscape and such.

But it was most imperative to spend some time this afternoon in appreciating the especially marvellous view. The most wonderful stretch of rail of all – one that you wish could continue for the whole journey – is that along Lake Baikal, through the enchanted woods that stretch up upon huge mountains unfathomable in the south, while the great lake glistens and glitters to the north like a boundless sea. One could be forgiven for thinking that it was a sea, sparkling in the sunshine as if in invitation to adventure, except for the occasional sight of faint, intriguing cliffs coming into view now and then on the other side. It has beautiful sands and people swim in it, I could see – but I could also see next to them lots of pollution gathered by the shore, so I wouldn't recommend it. Nonetheless, the beauty is unparalleled. When we swept around the edge of the lake and saw both lake and tree-clad mountains in the same view, t was mesmerising.

Tonight the landscape was flatter and more empty, and I missed the mountains already. I had my evening meal in the restaurant again. It was quite nice, but again not all that much for a main meal, and they charged me extra for requesting boiled rather than fried potatoes with my mushroom and tomato. I felt so tired, it was hard to stay up until the new 10 o' clock (which felt more like 11).

## Day 12: The Heart of Russia
*Wednesday 28th June*

*You are permitted to walk on the rails at Russian stations*

I shifted my clock back another hour today, to BST +5, the closest time to home since I arrived in Singapore over a fortnight ago. I had a restful night, lulled to sleep by the train's motion, and woke refreshed at 5 o' clock in this new time. Today the Trans-Siberian Express took us through flatter land, and a few large towns, but mainly enchanting woods. The golden light shifting through leafy boughs was tonight quite as beautiful as that seen in Worcestershire on sunny evenings at sunset at home. It was sunny for most of our westward journey, and already warm and bright in the Siberian summer for our first stop at 5:40, when I went for a walk.

We next stopped at about 10, when I enjoyed a proper 25-minute walk along the platform and up and down the stairs at a fairly large station that possessed a spectacular view of some mountains and contained a lot of old-fashioned lamp posts, which looked very charming. Again, people casually crossed the tracks so long as trains weren't coming, and I saw a train worker clinging to the front of one train while it moved. I was reprimanded for being a few seconds late back to the carriage (even though we still had 5 minutes left before departure) – our carriage attendant, a stern Russian woman, can be quite grumpy and strict. A man boarded the train who spent a lot of time with her and they were running the carriage together now – perhaps her lover?

All the station stop times are printed on notices in the carriages. My next chance to walk was at 4, at a place where clouds had gathered briefly and I felt a few spots of rain. This journey would be much less pleasant in the cold and wet of winter I'm sure! I was able to buy bananas and cherries there to boost up my fruit and vegetable intake. Then, I made sure to be back in good time. Really, though, only being able to walk briskly for one and a half hours each day is not ideal; it still felt a little like a self-imposed prison I now yearned to be free of. I'm never that comfortable sitting down for long periods, but nor is standing up for long comfortable on a train as one gets jolted about – and there are no opening windows to lean at like on the Intercity 125 back home. At least there is no air-conditioning on these trains, just a natural input of air as it flows past, which is much better for the environment, more pleasant and less frigid.

I was alone in my compartment again today, although the children from along the carriage did run in and make mischief from time to time. They wanted to hit each other with my books! I would like to be able to communicate – if only I'd found a Russian phrasebook. I spent nearly all the day reading and writing. Dante's 'Divine Comedy' was proving an inspiring read. I wrote another letter, and composed a work of fiction about such a train as this, hoping that this day was hence fruitful, though to simply stand and admire the beauty of creation is sufficient sometimes.

Russia is a beautiful, green land – in summer at least – with seemingly endless woods and streams. Occasionally a red and white power station chimney rears up its head from cities, but largely any pollution is hidden from view. The Trans-Siberian is an electric train, so at least is not polluting the immediate environment as it passes. There are some very rustic stations, where people appear sometimes with shopping trolleys full of goods, trying to sell you some. I cobbled together breakfast and lunch as usual, and again had the only vegetarian option of substance – potato and mushroom – in the restaurant car tonight. It was very quiet and the youngish waiter came to talk with me this time, which was mostly friendly, using his mobile telephone to translate. Some of what he said, though, was not so palatable – the gist of it seemed to be that the UK is debauched because it permits homosexuality. Were I a homosexual I might feel insulted and somewhat frightened; as it was, I was merely perplexed by such an odd thing to say. Old-fashioned views are evidently still current in Russia.

## Day 13: Western Russia
*Thursday 29th June*

*A Home for 6 days: On Board the Express*

Today, I changed to BST+4 – getting excitingly close to home, which meant I had a full, refreshing sleep in spite of rising at 5. Slow travel by land is certainly much better for your sleep patterns than travel by air – and you really can appreciate each hour gained or lost on the journey. The train stopped soon after I rose, giving time for a quick walk – you must take these opportunities while you can! I was able to wash my torso at least, despite being on a train, which at least made me feel relatively fresh for the new day. I felt very joyful and peaceful today, and was inspired to write another poem, which helped to pass the time.

I was still alone in my compartment – indeed, the train didn't fill up as we approached the end of the journey, and so it turned out I only had to share for one night of the six I was aboard. It is the festival of St Peter and St Paul, which added an air of celebration when I made my daily prayers. Today was also quite different from the others in that I spent nearly all morning reading and all afternoon writing. I have nearly finished reading Dante's Divine Comedy (you need a big, thick book like that to keep you occupied on the Trans-Siberian Express) and stood reading that at the end of the carriage; it's an enlightening, skilful and inspiring work; indeed, I missed reading it when it was finished!

Reading was necessitated by the landscape outside becoming a little more monotonous than it was in the dramatic earlier part of the journey. The train stopped at 12.10 for about 20 minutes, then we went on again with the same sorts of things passing by outside. I had my usual simple lunch – and some tea using the hot water that is available in carriages, still with the same paper cup I got in China. Looking at the gunk that's visible at the bottom of the transparent hot water tank, I wouldn't have wanted non-boiling water if it was on offer. This afternoon I was engrossed for some three hours in writing a little story about being on such a train as this. It added some imagined peril to the journey, and was quite enjoyable. Indeed, I was surprised that it was already time for another stop when it came, at 4.45 for nearly half an hour.

It was again very warm and sunny in Russia, but windier than of late today. I saw some lightning, but there was still plenty of sunshine into the evening, and the scenery continued to be beautiful, with lots of trees, meadows and green, grassy slopes between occasional towns. Russia is quite an underpopulated country, to say the least. The train braked very sharply tonight, but seemed to carry on again soon afterwards, unperturbed. I had my evening meal in the restaurant car again after 7, but they had now run out of potato (in Russia!) so I had to have only egg and tomato and a slice of bread, which did fine. I still had supplies of carrot and banana bought a few days ago.

The sunset was especially wondrous tonight, but it didn't occur until nearly 10, suggesting that another change of the clocks will be in order tomorrow. Not a great deal of excitement occurred today, I must admit, but such is the reality of life aboard a long-distance train.

## Day 14: Moscow
*Friday 30th June*

*Arriving into Moscow*

The final day aboard the Trans-Siberian Express! It was difficult to believe that it had been an entire week since I arrived in Beijing, so many days had been spent in this same compartment and carriage since then. Around five thousand miles had been traversed, across five time zones. I moved my clock to BST +3, getting still closer to home, and again rose at 5. We were actually fifteen minutes late, for the first time, for our first stop today which was supposed to be 5.51 and ended up being 6.06 – but they let us outside for five minutes anyway, which I rather felt in need of to stretch my legs!

I moved on to another book this morning, one on geopolitics I picked up at the start of my travels. It seems to paint global affairs in a rather negative light, as if wars are about to erupt everywhere. Perhaps they are, and perhaps the leaders of the nations should learn to trust each other more and stop competing so much – for instance, why is Russia given such a cold shoulder by the 'west'? It seems a quite pleasant place to me, but could be provoked if treated badly. We had another brief stop at about 12, giving me chance to top up my supplies for lunch. I switched to writing for the afternoon again, but somehow was not in such a creative mood today – I was excited, I suppose, about the prospect of finally reaching the end of this long, long journey!

Another 25 minute stop occurred at 3.30 at Vladimir, our last before Moscow. It was warm and sunny still – though not as hot as we had experienced further east – and I enjoyed some pleasant platform walks and seeing more of the preserved steam engines that used to run the line, which they still have (no longer working) at many of the stations. Our own electric engine was swapped there for a larger one. I don't know why; perhaps they have to be rested or checked after a certain distance. It had been cloudy and noticeably cooler earlier this morning, for the first time since I left Britain feeling noticeably chilly

The countryside is still vast, beautiful and green on approaching Moscow. As we neared the Russian capital, suddenly it began to rain heavily; with still over an hour ago I read some more of the '1001 Nights' I picked up in China, to transport me to Arabia. When, finally, we pulled into Moscow we were about 2 minutes late, which is rather good considering how far we had come! At last, I bade farewell to my home of the last six days, and stepped into yet another new city.

The rain stopped for just long enough for me to reach the nearest underground station, which I took as a sure sign that I should use it. Now, I had forgotten the exact name of my hotel and didn't know where to find it (don't forget that I brought no telephone or computer with me), but the first thing I saw in the underpass was a shop selling stationery – and, sure enough, maps. On one of these I saw the Hotel Ostankia listed in the directory, and recognised the name; by God's grace it just so happened to be located in a square of the map that could be seen through the cover without having to actually purchase the map, so I could see exactly which metro station to go to!

Metro line 1 I found to be quite shabby and difficult to negotiate; I changed, though, onto line 14 which looks brand new. As I was trying to find the hotel through a warren of streets, having alighted at the closest stop, heavy rain began again so I hid in another underpass. What is it with me and inviting the rain? I met it in Beijing too. When I found myself sheltering at a bus stop and still unsure of exactly where to go, the rain having started yet again, I hailed a taxi and it took me the last couple of miles for 200 roubles. It proved to be a good hotel, and after check-in I had a small but cheap evening meal, having eventually communicated the word 'vegetarian', of salad, a little bread and mashed potato. So to a proper bed tonight, at 10 Moscow time.

## Day 15: Belarus
### *Saturday 1st July*

*The Statue of Alexander I towers over Moscow*

It's two weeks now since I began my journey. I began this new summer month in Moscow, at last waking in a hotel rather than in a train again, and in BST +2. I was able to enjoy a proper shower to get thoroughly refreshed, before checking out of the pleasant hotel and walking back to the metro stop. No need for a taxi today; there was bright, warm sunshine, I now knew where to go and I found it not very far: it turned out I'd got the taxi when about half way to the hotel yesterday. I had a quick breakfast waiting for the metro, which is a cheap

55 roubles for the whole journey, and retraced the route on lines 14 and 1 I took yesterday, but this time went straight past the Trans-Siberian terminus to visit Revolutionary Place and the heart of Moscow.

It was quite amazing, and well worth the stop-off, to see the Kremlin in Red Square, the Cathedral of St Basil and Alexander I's huge monument. It is a beautiful, leafy and enjoyable city, but there is more poverty and homelessness here than I saw anywhere else on my journey, and I met several beggars. The fall of the USSR did have its downsides. I would not want to live in any of these big cities, but Moscow is certainly good to visit.

I couldn't stay very long (and spent some of the time buying supplies from what seemed a very posh supermarket compared to south-east Asia) before needing to catch the metro again. I took Line 1 from the Lenin Library then switched to Line 2 heading north to Belorusskaya station, from where I was to catch the 10.19 train to Berlin, via Belarus. The terminus stations are, of course, named after the lines that they serve. Belorusskaya is a pretty station.

When I'd found the right train (they very confusingly give both a platform and a 'track number' in Russia, and one doesn't always know at first which is which) I had to go right down to the front to find my sleeper compartment – the very front coach. The man I shared it with was very friendly and spoke some English so we talked for a bit, then I started to read. I have been rationing my political geography book as it is so enjoyable, and I fear to run out of reading material soon!

I read the chapter on China in China, that on Russia in Russia, and will read that on Western Europe tomorrow. There are also chapters on the Arctic and South America, places I can only imagine, but there is now much more of the world that I can accurately picture having visited it myself – the joys of long-distance overland travel!

Two women in the neighbouring compartment had an argument about whether to have the seats up or down (the sleeping position) so I was asked to swap with one of them. My new companions were a Russian chemistry student going to a conference in Cologne, who spoke English well, and an older woman who could only speak Russian and communicated with me via her. The older woman wanted to talk about politics and relations between Russia and the West, which I do wish could become more cordial: it is a wonderful country, and I think a lot of the distance between east and west is caused by the two sides actively antagonising each other for no reason. She was defending Crimea's annexation, arguing that its people are Russian anyway so there's no need to be up in arms about it. Whilst I don't defend the annexation, I do think that Russia and the West could have more sympathy for each other's point of view.

Our translator wasn't keen on talking politics, so we didn't talk about that for long. I spoke with her about climate change instead, something that interested us both. That all passed some time; I also exercised my brain on the cryptic crosswords in some tattered copies of the 'Big Issue' that I'd brought with me all the way from the UK. We stopped for 10 minutes twice, with a chance to walk – at Orska and Minsk in Belarus. For my meals I had bits and pieces that I had bought before we left, and the train café offered some extras to this. The staff seemed very friendly, quite a contrast to some of those on the Trans-Siberian. Outside was again a wonderful view, with bright sunshine, woods and seas of purple flowers. A mother and young child joined our compartment before nightfall, providing yet more opportunity to meet people and discover new perspectives.

*A Rainbow over Belarus*

## Day 16: Across Europe
*Sunday 2nd July*

*Early Sunday morning in Berlin*

It was again on a train that I awoke today, one final time. I was on the top berth of a full cabin; sleeping on the train is comfortable I find so long as you have somewhere to lie down. The young child in the compartment awoke us in the night a couple of times but it wasn't too bad. Waiting for customs between Belarus and Poland kept us up quite late anyway; the Polish officials came into the compartment and gave it a quick search. I'm used to that sort of thing by now!

This morning I was running on BST +1, feeling very close to home. We arrived in Berlin Oestbahnhoff at 7.20 having traversed Belarus and Poland, and were able to buy some breakfast there. I said farewell to the others in my compartment who were going on to Cologne, and myself went exploring Berlin. I'd visited once before, in 2010, and saw some of the same things that I did then, but this time the weather wasn't so pleasant: there was a chill breeze with sunny spells, as opposed to a heatwave back then. I felt cold, compared to the Asian climate! The metro connection to Hopfbahnhoff, where my next train was to leave from, took me through some quite shabby areas; Europe looks in some ways more run-down than the up-and-coming Asian cities.

At Hbf, I took a metro onwards to the Brandenburg Gate just to see it, for something to do, and found the tram almost deserted. I soon saw why: the Gate is in walking distance of the station, so taking the metro was quite unnecessary. Also, it was a Sunday morning, so even at the Brandenburg Gate there was nobody around. I had my breakfast there in the empty street, quite haunting really – only flocks of birds to be seen. I went to see the Holocaust memorial, always very moving, and the Reichstag from the outside – I see that nowadays there are more security measures there than there were in 2010, a sign of the changing times. I was able to have a good walk in the park nearby.

Then, back to the Hbf, where I had time to change some roubles to Euros before catching the 10:34 high speed train to Cologne. It seemed a long journey, the countryside grey and uninspiring outside, and I spent most of it standing up and reading. There was only 25 minutes at the busy station of Cologne – long enough to explore some of the very German-style stalls in the station and buy more supplies – before the 15.42 to Brussels. It seemed very fast indeed (200 mph), and I was glad the journey wasn't too long, having begun to tire after all these weeks of train travel.

We reached Brussels on time at 17.35, and I had another walk (not much to see) before going through customs at 6 ahead of catching the 18.56 train to London. Alas, there was a very long queue: all our bags had to be scanned, I had to take off my watch, belt and so on and it was all rather inconvenient – much more stringent than any of the other 7 borders I'd crossed since leaving Singapore. Passport control also took a long time and I was only just in time for the scheduled departure. However, we were delayed 25 minutes anyway waiting for people to board. Apparently this is all because security has very recently been tightened. Still, this was my first significantly delayed train of the whole trip.

It was a much newer train than I've been accustomed to on Eurostar; perhaps they replaced some of them recently. We stopped only at Lille, and I enjoyed looking out at the beauty of Belgian then – at long last – English countryside! It felt really quite fantastic to arrive at St Pancras, having travelled at 300 km/h on this last stretch of a long journey. I walked from there to Euston, it being such a lovely, sunny evening, with the wind and rain left far behind in Germany. From there, I took the underground to Paddington and was amazed at how much, much more expensive it is than the metro system in any of the Asian or European cities I've visited.

After all that travel, through so many different countries, over thousands of miles, it was inevitably at Paddington that I had my first hiccup. The Great Western Railway being its usual self, the train to Oxford was cancelled due to a signal fault. I was able to telephone home for the first time since Singapore (I'd only been able to email since) as in London at least there are still payphones. I caught the 21.42 train to Oxford, where I would stay overnight before going home to Worcestershire tomorrow. And that was that. Half way around the world over land in 16 days, 15 nights, going as quickly as possible by train. What an amazing journey it had been!

# SLOW TRAVEL

## AN ENVIRONMENTALIST'S ADVENTURE

*A fictional account of a journey around the world*

# Slow Travel:
## An Environmentalist's Adventure
*Introduction*

*Slow Travel* was written in a series of weekly segments for *The Poor Print* newspaper in Oxford between October 2015 and April 2018. It was a (mostly) fictional account of what was then the near future, set between 2018 and 2019. I style it now an 'environmentalist's adventure', because that is, in hindsight, what it was: an attempt to draw attention to the many environmental issues facing the world at that time, with many of the related social issues also touched upon. It is arranged, as it was originally published, in 30 episodes, each of which has a theme as well as describing a section of the journey. Four of these – 22 to 25 – are not fictional. They describe a true journey, the same *Singapore to London* adventure detailed in a more matter-of-fact manner in the first part of this book.

As I write, 2018 and 2019 are receding into the past: indeed three full years have elapsed since the fictional narrative ended. Some of my 'predictions' – such as a rail link between Russia and the USA, which was convenient for the narrative if somewhat unlikely – have not come to pass. I hope that readers will not be put off by this. Others, such as the election of Donald Trump as US president – which seemed equally unlikely in 2015 – did of course occur.

All the environmental issues highlighted in the travelogue are real, even if I have not visited in person the places concerned, information about which was gathered through various reputable sources on the internet and through environmental news outlets. Most if not all of them remain pressing issues today even as they were at the time of writing. Regardless of its originally intended date the travelogue continues to serve, therefore, as a reminder of the dire situation the world of our present age finds itself in as a result of a human failure to look after our natural environment or each other.

I hope that future readers will take some interest in these issues, and will find the narrative enjoyable. Perhaps, like me, you are impatient to see real action to stop the destruction of nature and the undermining of our own and other species' survival on this little gem of a planet. There has been some slight movement, I like to think, in this direction since the time when I wrote *Slow Travel*. With the advent of more extreme weather in almost every country environmental issues are at least making the headlines nowadays. But actions continue to fall short of words, and as time increasingly runs out for life on Earth as we know it, there seems no more prescient time to publish *Slow Travel* for the first time in a single printed volume.

# 1: Beginnings
*To London*

Forgive me if I start at the beginning. You might prefer to know the ending first, and judge from the conclusion whether setting out was worth my while at all. Or perhaps you'd rather have a taste, first, of the adventure that lies between the outset and the end, that you might survey the prospect from the highest peak of this the range of humble hills that is my tale, and know whether it will be worth your while to follow me on the lengthy climb and back. But the end can't be judged rightly, nor will the view be clear from the top, unless the purpose of my travels is first unfolded to your mind. Thus, you must forego for now these promised pleasures, trusting they'll be worthy of the effort spent obtaining them, and I shall begin at the beginning of my journey, and tell you why I first set out at all.

I began in the city. It was a cold spring morning; the light was soft, and probably, beneath wider skies, the countryside was thickly daubed in frost. Not here. Here, dirty puffs of steamy smoke leaked from the exhaust-pipes of at least a hundred humming cars. They grumbled, like impatient dogs eager to be let loose but, for now, constrained to crawl as a snaking stenchy dribble through the over-congested, stagnant city scape. I passed them briskly by, trying not to breathe the foul fumes or meet the eyes of the bored inhabitants – most of them alone in their little mobile spaces – sitting, picking noses, doing makeup, or simply frowning straight ahead at the long lines of angry red eyes peppering the road. Wasting time. Was it ever thus, I wondered. Since when had the city become the habitat of these glugging, jugging man-made beasts of burden? Was it really comfortable, locked within those private little shuttles of steel for minutes or hours on end? Wouldn't it be better to get up from those stymying seats and walk or ride together, in the open, to feel the wind and weather and to breathe the fresh air? At least, I reflected, coughing, they didn't have to breathe each other's fumes. Who knew what unnatural substances I harboured in my lungs, even now, collected over countless city walks?

I don't know when it happened – the place as it was then was all I had always known it to be – but I realised that that part of the city, for all its light and noise and people, had been dead for a long time.

Still, I wouldn't dwell there in its putrid corpse for much longer. I crossed a grey and lifeless concrete bridge, and made my way up to the station. At least there was life here, amidst the bustle and hurry outside the main station entrance. A heartfelt burst of laughter peeled from a café; a litter-picking street-cleaner whistled as he passed, picking up another twenty-first century gem with his tweezers. So carelessly discarded, it would be destined, no doubt, for some hole in the countryside, where it could rest and rot as the centuries passed: a record in perpetuity of what we were today. But most people were locked up in their own little worlds, dreaming perhaps of people, places and ideas far away from that man-made desert of concrete and grime. Only a Big Issue vendor, alone in having nowhere else to hurry to, implored them all to come back down to this little patch of Earth. Ignored. They carried on in silence, or talking in their own small companies. They didn't see the world around them; they didn't see it changing, slowly slipping away. They were all too busy, without the time to stop and think of where that cigarette end would end up they'd tossed upon the floor, or whence came that plastic bottle bought and drained and flung upon the pile growing by the minute atop the litter-bin.

But I had time. I'd left nearly an hour to catch my train. I bought a magazine, buoyed up by the friendly smile of one so pleased to sell it. Then I stood and watched on platform 3 while the trains came and went, and a thousand lives crossed mine just for a moment, waiting for the slow train to London and on to Paris. Yes, I had time. I was, as I call it, 'travelling slow'.

The world – that is, both our human world, and the nature that surrounds us – wasn't well. So I had been told. Not that I myself had ever known it significantly different, had known it to be 'well', so to speak. Nor had I witnessed personally the frightening changes reported to be taking place across the entire globe. But I did know by instinct – in common, I think, with all empathetic beings – what was most beautiful, most wonderful, most meaningful about our world. I knew, too, what was most alien and unpleasant but, for a time at least, to be endured within it. And the reports I was hearing certainly worried me. They suggested that the wonderful was losing out to the alien like never before. Though I hadn't known a planet covered in forests, which is what I was told had existed millennia before, I did know and love trees as beautiful beings to live alongside and for the peace, reassurance and life-giving air they exuded, and I knew that the net loss of billions per year could not be good. I loved the wonderful diversity of life in Earth, and I felt that the extinction of so many plants and animals that thrived in these forests as their paradise degraded into wasteland was a sorrow quite unbearable. For the climate in which all this fantastic life had flourished and adapted – not just in forests but right across our beautiful world – to change seemed a travesty; for once life-full, verdant lands and oceans to be littered with lifeless synthetic creatures seemed a disgrace.

Soon, the reports implied, humanity would be doomed to breathe an alien atmosphere with alien weather, walking on alien ground amidst alien seas, and the garden that had sustained us in lives of love and joy was to be uprooted. I could not take these tales for granted; I had to see and know for myself what was occurring to believe that such an apocalypse could really soon be unleashed. And there you have it: the purpose of my travels. But the tale of my beginnings is not yet quite complete.

Had I but wished to see the destruction of our planet at first hand, I had it within my means to soar from place to place by plane with the greatest speed. I could witness in a week the burning of the forests, the lives blighted by pasture become desert and slowly-rising seas beyond my control. But the greatest tragedy, of all that I had heard, was that the sickness in the world around me was not out of my control at all. I had caused it – we had caused it; it was bred of a sickness within my own society that had taken hold long before my birth and was driving us to destroy our very selves. The fact that the lungs of the world were being shredded, the lands and oceans wasted, the air poisoned and the people made miserable not by natural accident but by active human hands, gripped by a fever of envy and greed, was the hardest to bear at all. And the desire for instant, world-wide travel was, I realised, one of the most destructive symptoms of this foul disease. So I did not set out only to see the changing world; I set out to change it myself, if only in my own tiny, perhaps insignificant capacity, hoping that – like the flap of a butterfly's wings that seeds an entire storm – my little choices might grow somehow in influence to have a large effect. So I wasn't going to dash with greedy haste from place to place by air. I was going to travel slowly, reverently, over land and sea, and see for myself what the world is and was and could become from the point of view of the slow journeyman, who alone can live and breathes and truly know each landscape. This was my beginning down a slowly-trammelled path.

## 2: Digitality
*From London to Paris*

'Could I have your number, please?' said the young woman behind the desk. Her hands hovered over her keyboard in anticipation.

'My number? What number?' I asked, feeling somewhat perplexed. After all, it was getting late in the evening and the weariness of a long day's travelling lay upon me.

'Your telephone number,' she said in her impeccable English accent.

'I don't have a telephone,' I replied. She looked surprised.

'Then how can we text you your ticket?' she said. 'Perhaps we can send it by email – what is your email address?'

'Well I don't have a computer – not any more,' I replied.

Now she looked worried. 'We need a telephone number or an email address to send the ticket,' she insisted. 'Are you sure you don't have a telephone?'

Was I sure? A ridiculous question. But this wasn't the time to argue. I was trying to book onto a train that would take me onwards through Europe the very next day. So I conjured up my old email address – which should still work. Satisfied, she smilingly typed it in. Clearly, I was going to have to find an internet café somewhere in Paris the next morning.

As usual, I set out to walk the city before dawn. At that time of the day, when darkness still clings to deserted boulevards and alleyways, and even stars sometimes poke through in pockets where the glaring orange blindfold of the streetlights is torn, every city takes on a special character. Devoid of the incessant chatter and clatter, ticking engines and wailing horns that mar each flustered, in-a-hurry day, an ancient tranquillity creeps back in beneath those eternal celestial watchers of the night. At times, early busses whoosh by like swooping owls; here and there a fellow shadow wanders the resting, deserted stones. But largely, for a short time at least, a lonely serenity reigns.

Then slowly, almost imperceptibly, the footfalls increase, and life returns to greet the rising sun. It is a comfort that, even in this digital age, one primeval animal instinct largely survives: the glare of screens and speakers has not yet drowned the quiet call of the sun by day and moon or stars by night bidding us to wake or rest. And, after the earlier solitude, it warms the heart to see and hear people of all ages and professions giving of their boundless walking, talking, breathing energy to replenish the vibrancy of this busy capital. Each clatter of the metro, each snatch of birdsong resounding from the neatly-arrayed tall trees, each snippet of French conversation wafting, with the smell of freshly-brewed coffee, from each quiet café: all make this the living, human place it is. Or at least, that's how it used to be.

But nowadays, the streets begin to clog more quickly and the hoot of horns soon returns. As I make my way into the city's heart, I pass the silent congregations gathering round bus-stops, their heads bowed as if in prayer at some mournful funeral. Theirs is no reverential gesture: their ears are stopped, their eyes are focussed down upon the garish, flashing screens they cradle, too distracted by their digital preoccupations to watch the waking day. And I, though in the midst of such a busy crowd, feel utterly alone. For whom, amongst these digital people, has eyes to see and ears to hear the world around them any more?

Soon the great Notre Dame rises into my sight, that towering ancient testament of love and past enchantment that carries my thoughts away to a time when Christianity so perfused the lives of those that dwelt here that they mustered all their industry and ingenuity to assemble this incredible monument. Nowadays it's hidden from afar, lost betwixt the frowning faces of later, taller towers that have crowded out the shrine of love with one of money, the slave-driver of today's faster world. These were built in months; in years perhaps they'll fall. But the house they hide, constructed as much by centuries of prayer as by stone and mortar, will outlive them all.

Yet, as I enter, I find it difficult to hear the echoes of those countless prayers recited down the years. Now, the place is thronged with tourists who look not with their eyes but with their hand-held camera-'phones, which they wave throughout the building in a forest of fluorescence. I wonder whether they don't, in their eagerness to capture for the future the beauty they behold, lose it not only for the present but altogether. For how many of these photographs would ever meet their eyes again? And which amongst them could ever convey the true awe and majesty of the place which they, through the very act of taking pictures, only worked to dispel for those of us not looking through digital eyes? There was little tranquillity to be found amidst that fleeting, photo-stopping crowd.

It took me a little while to find an internet café. They used to be so common, not very long ago, at a time when to enter the world of the digital one would need to seek out one of its portals and, when finished, could simply shut the door and walk away. No longer: now it follows us everywhere, demanding our attention. Few places are immune from the ever-loudening drum of digitality, beating incessantly through a million mobile telephones and 'tablets' which people cling to like cherished children, never sleeping, always wailing for the attention of their twittering guardians.

Running Windows XP on a screen like a small cupboard, the cafe computer was hopelessly out-of-date compared to those machines. But it printed me my ticket, quickly and efficiently. Switching it off, I looked around the shadowy room, at first glance a quintessentially old-fashioned French place. But yes, here too the multiplying machines had made their habitation. In the corner, a couple sat in silence, each with a mobile telephone before them, their heads down, reading messages or chuckling to themselves. Only when the waiter arrived did they look up and converse. As they spoke, he whipped out a PDA and began to tap in their order. How long will it be, I wondered, before we forget how to write altogether? By the window a bored little girl slowly slurped through a straw, her father typing frantically on the touch-screen on his table. Work, play and conversation follow you everywhere, now. Some call it freedom. I call it slavery.

I didn't give the waiter chance for further practice on his PDA; it was time to amble back to the station. The little girl smiled at me as I left. Her father did not look up. I sighed to think that this was the city where, in December 2015, so many promises were made. Two years on, the people were more plugged-in and wired-up than ever, often I saw them apparently talking to themselves as they walked the streets. A decade ago it would have turned heads. It's no wonder all those promises are coming to nothing: with every gram of precious metal mined, every Watt of energy wasted to feed these ever-hungrier handheld devices, the planet gets just a little warmer. And, each lost in our own digital universe, we cannot hear the ticking clock, nor see the gathering clouds.

# 3: Translation
## *From Greece to Egypt*

With the Mediterranean Sea shimmering silkily around me in the soft spring sunlight, it is difficult to believe that there could ever be anything but peace and tranquillity between those quiet coasts, blessed with a beauty beloved since ancient times and hardly diminished in our own. As if in some delicious dream of mesmerising mountains and idyllic isles, I slowly slip across that dazzling space. Alas, it is no longer possible to glide – as centuries of seafarers had done before me – with only the power of the wind upon my sails or oars licking the water pushing me on. But I have boarded the smallest, slowest ferry I can find, meandering my way from Greece to Egypt via several island stops.

The engine's hum is quiet, and the glitter of solar panels of the cabin roof reminds me that at least some thought was being given to the need to use energy sparingly and efficiently if we are to preserve this precious world of life. And yet, I know, such gestures aren't enough. What difference will a few solar panels – or 'energy-saving' lightbulbs or 'fuel-efficient' cars for that matter – really make? None at all, if they simply tempt us to plug in more and more powerful electronic devices, not bother to switch of the lights or make more journeys by car. Such is the fallacy of 'energy efficiency'. And a little bit of tinkering with a few boats bobbing on the Mediterranean cannot save us if the planes I see above me continue to streak like high-flying hawks across the blissful blue sky.

But climate change is far from the thoughts of the people here. Beyond a few grumbles about the fishing stocks not being what they were, they seem content that their sea and islands continue to thrive, so it seems, as lusciously as ever. But these are not the islands their ancestors knew – not really. Urbanity and Industry have a long history here, but the roads and cars that cut across and the myriad new villas and apartments that crowd out the ancient tranquillity of this sublimely cultural constellation represent a fundamental shift in the quality of the habitat here on which life in all its forms depends to flourish.

And still more change is coming, of a still less intentional kind. You can almost see it, rolling in like the storm-clouds that gather, at first in mere hints and whispers of shadows on the horizon, before with cruel rapidity the tranquil sea collapses into a cauldron of chaos. Storms are coming from many directions. As we approach the island of Crete, I think of the many olive-growers there who wait with baited breath, hoping that the disease that has devastated the centuries-old olive-trees of Italy, having been translated inadvertently by humans from the Americas, doesn't make the further leap to strip their fertile isle, too, of its most precious produce. But if the ships and planes keep moving, it's only a matter of time.

Yet it is human translation that poses the bigger threat. Everywhere here there are memories of the refugees who struggled across these waters in 2015, desperately seeking salvation from the suffering of needless war and persecution blighting their own countries. Then, migrating people poured through these ports, and many lost their lives on these seductive seas. At the time of my travel, the Greeks are glad that this crisis has abated, but I don't think they realise that, because of climate change, this is just the beginning. As the world warms and seas rise, swathes of Africa and Asia will become uninhabitable, and then not thousands but millions of people will be displaced. Europe, where – misled by the sugar-coated 'medicine' of capitalist rhetoric – many elsewhere have come to believe the very streets are paved with gold, will be the destination of which they dream. And everything the people here still hold onto from their past – the last pockets of natural peace, the cultural artefacts – may well be lost in the translation.

I arrive in Alexandria as the sun begins to sink, and all around bright lights sprinkle streets and high-rise buildings. For over two millennia this city has thrived at the centre-point of moving goods and people, the gateway to Egypt, its culture and resources. But is it really all that 'Egyptian' any more? Did not these street-lights and skyscrapers originate with European and American planners and architects, trying to transform their own cities far away? How, then, did these ugly edifices come to be here? The Egyptians could craft buildings befitting their harsh environment thousands of years ago. The Pyramids of Giza, the Lighthouse and

Library of Alexandria were Wonders of the Ancient World. Now air-conditioning units struggle to keep cool constructions designed in other places but carried here by capitalists. They desire to exploit the whole wide world, to 'develop' this country in ways that profit the rich but, unlike those ancient wonders, bring little lasting benefit.

Although decorated with hieroglyphs, to me the concrete face of the new library at Alexandria seems just another alien blot on an increasingly ink-spilt skyline. Does this truly invoke the ancient splendour of Egypt, this modern-day megalith that might sit just as easily, barring a few decorations, in London, Sydney or New York?

At least in Alexandria I found preserved some snatches of authentic Egyptian life not buried by foreign bulldozers. But it was on arrival at Cairo, after a long hot journey mostly by slow boat along the Nile, that I was truly struck by the grim reality of the devastation wrought through so-called 'development'. The river itself brewed with warnings as I approached. That life-blood of the ancient kingdom, which long ago was cherished, protected and even worshipped with such reverence, now stank with the filth of industrial pollution. But the city, sitting like a fat black spider at the end of its dirty thread, went beyond anything I had experienced before. A poisonous smog hung in the air, belched out by scores of metal-working factories. That this desert location had been exploited by artificial means far beyond its natural capacity to support humans was evident all around. The sewers overflowed in poorer areas packed with people; smoky motorcars jammed the streets. Perhaps this didn't bother the rich, ensconced within more ivory towers of alien glass and steel while beneath them people struggled to live in a poverty perpetuated by their greedy, profit-driven practices.

The tourists, of course, trod only the richer paths, opiated by token cultural treasures preserved for their benefit. But capitalism is eating away at Egypt, as it is so much of the world. With its money-minting steamroller it has crushed culture into conformity, paradise into pollution, sustainability into cataclysm and contentment into greed. We can see it in the languages lost year by year as traditional societies surrender to homogeneity. Your culture and your language are intricately intertwined. And, just as for a lost language, once you lose your culture you can't translate it back.

## 4: Force

Travelling slowly into the Holy Land, I tread a path taken by countless millions of pilgrims before me, congregating here from every direction. A peculiar power dwells in this small corner of the world, on the Fertile Crescent where human civilisation first found its genesis. A force draws people here – some in peace, some in war – to holy ground that has felt the feet of myriad preaching prophets and countless clashing armies. It's a landscape wildly transformed by human society. The land, once so fertile and flush with forests, was degraded by centuries of constant use, and long ago its ancient civilisations declined in prominence, to be conquered by the Persian, Roman, Islamic, Christian and modern European Empires that have all felt the pull of this place and desired to take it for themselves. But its inhabitants have resisted them all, often violently, and as I approach the border of this long-contested country, I find it still wracked by war. Barriers between cultures become physically tangible here where the deep trench of segregation between Palestinian natives and Israeli colonists is made hideously manifest in fences and walls.

Approaching from Egypt, it would be perilous and probably futile to attempt to pass through the Palestinian-administered enclave of Gaza. As I gaze at the high, wired fences that ring it round, 'prison' seems to me a more fitting description. To protect the state of Israel from the fearless force of fanatical Palestinians who attack their perceived oppressors, sometimes suicidally, a counter-force of fences is deemed a necessary evil. The freedom of the few is sacrificed for the security of the many in a trade-off that speaks loudly of the severe sickness of heart that has infected this place. The officials at the Egyptian-Israeli border are uncompromising. Had I been a professed Muslim or an Arab, the crossing would be near-impossible. Fortunately, I pass through without any greater difficulty than the Israeli stamp on my passport, a mark brandished here with pride but which, I reflect, will rule out any chance of entering Syria or Lebanon. It is a suspicious tension, not the Peace of God, which seems to prevail over the Holy Land I witness.

Jerusalem. The Holy City gleams before me, the focus of the three Abrahamic faiths and the centrepiece, it would appear, of God's communication with mankind. It still possesses a power, beyond that of any other city, to move the mind, heart and soul of many a pilgrim arriving at its walls. In the Old City temples, minarets and spires jostle with one another, shimmering in the sunlight like a golden desert oasis amidst the arid hills. The place where Christ was crucified, where Muhammad made his Night Journey; the city Richard the Lionheart wept to see but not to enter, and from which countless composers of words, paint and music have drawn their enlightened inspiration. My breath, too, was taken as I looked down from the dusty Biblical hills that crown this ever-treasured gem and felt for myself the glowing embers of a powerful past.

Attacked fifty-two times over its history, this jewel is still contested, and both Israelis and Palestinians claim it for their own. Another great barrier fences Jerusalem's eastern side, separating Israel from the Palestinian West Bank in the east. Though it will still be possible for me to travel on to the blessed city of Bethlehem, somewhere over the hazy horizon, the concrete and wire fencing ensure these two spiritually significant cities are more forcefully cut asunder than ever before.

In the Old City still stands the great Western Wall of the Jewish Temple, a testament to a conflict waged here nearly two millennia ago when, in the meeting of Jewish insurrection with the full force of Roman Imperial power, the great building was destroyed. Now it is the Israeli state's fear of Arab insurrection that pulls a pall of watchful, wary tension over this place of prayer. As I climb the Temple Mount, passing through the army of policemen that guards it, I think of the words that lie at the heart of those religions that hold this site so sacred, words that must have been spoken here countless times before. 'Hear, oh Israel, the Lord our God is one Lord: and thou shalt love the Lord thy God with all thine heart and with all thy soul and with all thy might'. Taken on its own, it would be tempting to see this as the source of the uncompromising, all-consuming religion that divides this land's people by creed and culture to the point of death. And yet, just as important in all these religions stands its companion commandment, 'and thou shalt love thy neighbour as thyself.' The first cannot be accomplished without the second, and that this commandment has so clearly not been put into practice by the neighbouring peoples here speaks more of a human inability to truly 'love the Lord' than it does about any supposed divine origin for the man-made religious divisions that mar this region.

Crossing the concrete wall that scars this now so severely deforested, unnatural landscape, I wonder how often the perpetrators of war stop to ponder the wider-reaching effects of their actions. Every bomb, whether detonated by incensed fundamentalists or dropped in the name of 'counter-terrorist' war, comprises a concoction of deadly chemicals designed to cause death. As well as snatching away lives and ruining landscapes by battering one another with these brutal inventions, the warring powers waste vast resources and pollute our precious planet even by manufacturing such monstrosities. How much suffering, future conflict and fundamentalism will be fuelled by climatic change accelerated by the armadas of aeroplanes and armies engaged in modern war? In fighting one another to impose short-term security by force, we only condemn ourselves to centuries of calamity. From the perspective of this timelessly sacred city, today lapped by the surging seas of short-sighted war, it all seems so pointless.

The Jordan River valley leads me to a sorrowful end of my slow journey through the Holy Land. The crystal waters of the life-giving river in which Christ himself was baptised are no more; now the flow is filthy, sluggish and subdued, composed entirely of sewage and a salty slime disgorged by fish ponds. Hostility between the nations through which the Jordan flows has led to each piping off what it can for irrigation, with none taking responsibility for the protection of the ecosystems that, even through all the conflicts that have plagued this region over previous millennia, until now flourished on this artery of life. That was before man declared war on his own mother, Nature. The Jordan's Dead Sea discharge is become a pathetic deathly dribble, this wonderful force of nature is so severely sapped. Now the Sea, as never before, is worthy of its name. This shrinking, shrivelled swamp is mankind's foremost mark upon the landscape to which we owe our civilisation's genesis; greed has supplanted gratitude it seems. And as I leave this elegiac Holy Land, the prospects of peace and prosperity seem furthest from my sight. This land of our salvation was, and is, also the site of our species' greatest sins.

## 5: Extortion
*From Saudi Arabia to UAE*

Down the dusty road from Jordan into Saudi Arabia I make my slow but steady way. The bus takes me southwards through this dry desert peninsula, on another route frequented by pilgrims from far and wide down the ages. They travel in their millions to Mecca and Medina – those great, ancient outposts of vibrant civilisation in the midst of an arid land – which complete the trio of holy sites, so curiously but perhaps meaningfully clustered on this narrow bridge between Africa, Asia and Europe, that have historically been thronged in religious festivals of global importance. Unlike their northern cousin, Jerusalem the besieged and divided, to this day these cities continue to witness an annual swelling of their populations by several times at the appointed time of year.

I am glad not to be travelling during the Hajj, when these roads will be packed with pilgrims beyond counting: a wonderful and inspiring sight, to be sure – especially in an age of apathetic secularisation when such meaningful and committed sacrifice of time, effort and home comforts for the sake of one's core purpose and belief is rare – but nevertheless not the safest place for a slow traveller to be caught amidst the rushing crowds. One wonders whether the commandment to do pilgrimage – given at a time when the Muslim world was smaller and travel was more spiritually reverential and less harmful to the environment – should really still

102

apply across the world today, or whether the meaning of this once so humble, arduous pilgrimage is lost amidst the bustle of modernity. I am glad, too, not to be here in high summer, when today's sweltering maximum temperature of nearly forty degrees could easily be topped by another ten. Even here in the relatively cool coastal mountains of the west, the sun beats a parched and weary heat from hot horizon to hot horizon and the very air feels heavy to my unaccustomed lungs.

Regular temperatures much higher than this would simply not be survivable, and it is ironic that things will only get worse as the climate changes, further scorching a country that, more than most, has hinged its economic survival on the very fuel that fires global warming. Saudi Arabia is almost utterly dependent on oil. Extorting this black gold from the Earth accounts for ninety per cent of its exports and almost its entire domestic production and service industries. It far exceeds the country's extortion of water, which is mostly derived from non-renewable aquifers now four-fifths exhausted by a small but significant unsustainable domestic agriculture. But environmental sustainability isn't top of the agenda here, and I'm surprised that even talking about climate change hasn't been declared illegal by the oligarchic regime that's getting rich from global warming. After all, reporting on poverty – another important subject – has been banned, and the government refuses to acknowledge that it even exists, or to gather any statistics on how many of the exploited lower classes are failing to benefit from its oil-fired boom.

Medina greets me like a microcosm of all this: a dream-like mountain 'paradise' sprouting from the parched earth, flourishing civilisation where there ought to be desert. At the end of a shimmering ribbon of road, the city seems at first a magical and welcoming sight but, in common with much of modern Saudi Arabia, its charms are superficial – artificial, even, manufactured in the image of the rich world that it apes. There are mosques, domes and minarets aplenty amidst the modern skyscrapers and apartments, but one would be mistaken to imagine that these reflect the ancient heritage of the city. Most of the centuries-old monuments hereabouts are no longer standing. Considered idolatrous under the strict religion of the Saudi government, many shrines, Mosques and places associated with the Prophet Muhammad have been destroyed in the past few decades lest they become the foci of idolatrous worship of places and people rather than God. It's a point of contention that's surfaced many times in religious history: do devotional images and buildings draw us closer to God or distract us from Him? Often, though, this sort of violent iconoclasm speaks more of the ruling regime's desire to demonstrate its own power and impose its own man-made religion on its subjects than of selfless sacrifice to God. Amidst the foreign fabrications of Medina – or at least, those parts that a 'non-Muslim' is permitted to visit – I feel little connection with the past and little sense of peace.

I find greater peace in the mountains away from the city, and the next few days see me journey slowly, by foot and by bus, from their majestic, spiritual splendour down towards the hot, flat plains of the east. It is too hot to travel in the middle part of each day, and I take advantage of my long sojourns in villages and towns to sample at least a taste of a past, nomadic culture that is being slowly suffocated beneath the wasteful and exploitative Saudi Arabia of today. There is, still, some wildlife to be seen here, though the desert's biggest creatures – onyx, leopard and gazelle – were wiped out by the over-extortionate hunting of the mid-twentieth century. When I eventually reach the capital Riyadh it strikes me as profoundly uninspiring. Adorned now with ostentatious trappings designed to flaunt the greedy, excessive wealth of the rich oil barons, there is very little left of the town's humbler beginnings. If Mecca and Medina are the region's spiritual heart, Riyadh is a temple to the gods of money and material wealth, and gives perhaps a truer illustration of where the hearts of the ruling classes lie. At least, though, I saw there one small nod towards sustainability in the recycling of sewer water to quench the city's thirst.

It's difficult to see any such signs at my next major stop, just across the border: the city that shouldn't be. I reach Dubai on the coast road by air-conditioned coach, which gives a strong foretaste of the city itself: artificially ice-cool where it should be burning hot. Here, capitalist competition for show-offish success and disregard for the long-term prosperity of the planet meet their crux amidst the world's tallest buildings, which rise from the dust like Towers of Babel. The huge airport – which forms a brief stopping-point for countless fast travellers on their thoughtless long-distance journeys – provides the best indication I know of for the extortionately fast pace of the modern world. The air-conditioned buildings, the ice rink in the desert, the fake sand on fake islands on a man-made coastline: all strive to keep up the pretence that so many people living here is normal.

But the resource costs of keeping all these wealthy residents and tourists not only alive but drowning in material excess are huge. The city lives off non-renewable extortion of natural resources and human labour like nowhere else. Dubai is mankind saying to itself, 'look at my greatness, thriving even in the harshest of environments'. Yet it can't last. If the planet takes this trajectory, it can't be long before our own Ozymandian ruins give testament to the foolishness of our pride. And looking on at all these mighty modern works, I myself almost, indeed, despair.

# 6: Ritual

It was with some trepidation, given the Israeli stamp on my passport, that I entered the port of Dubai to board a boat to Iran. It's ironic that in the interlinked world of today borders are more sharply defined and suspiciously watched than ever, so that it's no longer possible to travel freely, like our ancient ancestors on their long, slow trek out of Africa, even by foot over 'national borders'. The rigidly defined nation-state was a foreign idea even to Europeans only a few centuries ago, when one's allegiance lay more with one's own city, village or region than with the king and country. Now, in the wake of the colonial and, later, capitalist empires, it's become a convention universally imposed.

But as it transpires, my apprehensions are needless. This is 2018, and fortunately this particular border has seen restrictions slacken over recent years. Iran's icy stand-off with the west has been thawing, gradually, for some time now, as the country eagerly seeks to encourage a growing tourist industry. I obtained my travel visa months in advance, and besides, I'm taking the easy route in – via Kish Island.

As I ferry steadily across the glistening blue water, it isn't difficult to discern that Kish is no paradise – at least, not by any definition I'd countenance. If I had taken Dubai to be the shiniest plastic jewel in the capitalist crown I was about to be rudely re-educated. For Kish is nothing other than a giant luxury shopping and holiday resort, the true Queen of Consumerism.

Over my head the planes pour in as the richest ranks of Asia gather to splash their grotesque gluts of cash, on a modern-day pilgrimage to the man-made Mecca of Money. This is not a place in which I can bare to stay long: an island full of people piously performing their ritual sacrifices to the never-dead religion of worldly pleasure. Ritual buying, ritual consuming, ritual craving – on and on the capitalist cycle turns, consuming their lives and, with its superficial satisfactions, hiding the silent sufferings of the soul.

Ever has it been thus, since man first fashioned for himself gods of wood and stone and bowed the knee before his own creations. Religions of ritual providing easy answers to the questions of life and throttling thought; easy means of holding power over a people by promising happiness in return for a few simple actions. Sacrifice this ox, worship this golden calf, buy these new 'consumables' to keep the economy growing – it all has the same effect. There's no need to think or question, only to obey.

There are few places more religious than Iran. I don't mean by this a personal piety amongst its inhabitants, or any special degree of faith or enlightenment in its people, something that would be difficult for an outsider to assess. Rather, it's the officialdom of religion here that's so striking. Humans in all places, of all ethnicities, possess a common capacity for weakness of spirit and succumbing to selfish temptations, and the very public religiosity of the Iranian state profoundly demonstrates this weakness whatever the true beliefs of its subjects. Prophets, in their many guises, have lived and died to show humankind the secrets of good religion – practises grounded in empathetic love, tolerance and contemplation. And yet, as I step from another ferry onto the sandy shores of the Iranian mainland, I find myself in a country that, in the name of one such prophet, imposes a strict religiosity that has nothing to do with his compassionate message and everything to do with worldly power.

I carry no camera on my slow travels, and here it is just as well. The Iranian state is deeply suspicious of anything that might constitute an internal or external threat to its Draconian government, and photography of anything but obvious tourist attractions could cause trouble. I do not fancy the life of a foreign 'spy' in an Iranian jail. Likewise, 'western' films and music are heavily restricted lest they encourage free thought and expression. Despite the sweltering heat, long sleeves are compulsory; were I a woman, I'd also have to cover my hair.

Yet whatever the government may desire, and whatever images may filter through the negative 'western' media, the minds of the people of this mythical land are far from closed. Sharing a meal in a local guest-house, I hear for myself some of the fables that still run through the very blood of this ancient caring people, who treat each weary traveller with a selfless hospitality. It was in these very hills that Zoroastrianism was founded, an ages-old source of enlightened revelation.

'Iran' is an ancient word for what we once called 'Persia', and its adoption as the country's name in 1935 reflects an ongoing pride in a not-forgotten heritage more than two millennia after the mighty Persian Empire fell with the rise of Greece and Rome. But it is the Islamic Empire that has held the most lasting sway of all upon this people, and through day-to-day acts of kindness is their true 'submission to the will of God' displayed.

I have arrived at the beginning of the holy, ritual month of Ramadan, and so we eat our meal after sunset and prayer. The state marks this month by banning eating, drinking and smoking in public outright. But the true spirit of the Muslim fast lies only within its genuinely willing adherents. You can see it in their eyes in these difficult early days: the hunger and the inner struggle they all must make. But in their kindly words and actions the people that I meet show few outward signs of fasting. The benefit of this ritual lies in private piety, not public pomp, for any true Muslim.

The government – except to display its own power – really has no need to enforce the Ramadan ritual. Indeed, the Iranian Christians, Jews and others, with their own rituals and traditions, can only be hampered by enforced outward conformity. I meet few of these on my onward journey through the rugged mountain towns; though there are three-hundred-thousand Christians in Iran, conversion from Islam can be punishable by death. Most of my travel is by train, on the slow line winding north from the coast through Sirjan to Bafq, and thence east along a brand new, shiny

110

stretch of rail to Zahedan and on to Pakistan. I alight often to breathe in the fresh mountain air and hear the chatter of an unfamiliar tongue.

In places, amidst the mesmerising Middle-Eastern architecture, it feels as though I walk through the remnants of a former world, almost overlooked by modernity in its hasty spread across the globe. But one can't help wondering whether this reflects genuine reverence for tradition or compulsory conformity, and the very presence of the railway hints at change to come. As I look out from the ageing carriage window, with majestic mountains sweeping down towards the pretty plains and desert, I reflect that somewhere, still, out there Iranian cheetahs dwell. But the lions and tigers of old were chased out by the twentieth century. Which of these ancient rites and rituals will be buried by the twenty-first?

## 7: Green
### *From Pakistan to India*

The Hunza Valley stretches out before me, reposing upon my vision like a verdant dream. Except that no dream could conjure such sparkling, vivid colours, nor invoke such unimagined beauty as that possessed by this high Green Heaven. Around it, a crisp crown of snow-capped mountains dazzles in the shimmering summer sunlight, completing the perfect picture of a true paradise. It was worth the long, slow climb into the Karakorum, high above the plains of Pakistan, to find this overawing treasure at the top. Yet the genesis of Hunza is a story more subtle than it might at first appear. For how could such a haven of fertility flourish amidst these rocky, barren heights? The truth is that these trees, these flowers, these fruits and fields of plenty are all mankind's making – the happy result of humans working hand-in-hand with Nature, for once, to bring a landscape alive.

Centuries ago, the ancient Hunza people, who until then had relied on raiding and plunder to survive where sustenance was scarce, carefully carved out canals at just the right inclination to carry meltwater from the glacier to quench their thirsty fields: a natural flow diverted through human skill. Hidden in their mountain home, they remained for decades an isolated but self-sustaining, prosperous community, blessed with the joys of a simple life in their lofty Eden.

Ascending to the valley in 2018, I find that little has changed. I come as one of a small but growing number of travellers and tourists who take the long road, by bus or on foot, into these magnificent mountains, to climb the slopes or simply look upon an unspoiled green ambrosia now so rare in the world. The people are gracious and giving, well-educated in spite of their remote position, and seemingly in a state of near-perfect contentment, the secret of joyful life that humanity once held but let slip from its grasp. Having all the simple things they want or need, they crave for nothing more. My visit here has filled my own heart with a joy unparalleled, and it is with refreshed inspiration that I take my leave and begin my descent towards the plains. If only that 'green' vision – that sustainable contentment and reverence for nature – pervaded our world more widely, I wonder wistfully, could we not all live in such peaceful bliss?

But greed, not gratitude, is the attitude that prevails in most of the corporate-controlled world that I witness, and there is little such enlightenment in lowland Pakistan. A bus carries me south into the country's agricultural heartland, the largest area of artificially irrigated cropland in the world, and a monument to the 'Green Revolution' imposed by the British in colonial times. The Empire greened the Indus desert by taming the mighty rivers of the Punjab – literally, the 'land between five rivers' – in their greedy thirst to expand their cotton plantations. This was no careful, reverent re-direction like that carried out in the

Hunza hills, but an industrial-scale onslaught of over-irrigation that, over the decades, has released a deadly poison in the soil they sought to enrich: salt. At the edges of the farms and fields, a vast swathe of white death encroaches year by year, land spoiled by a rising water-table that has dragged up this demon from the deep. Entering this man-made wilderness is stepping onto an alien world, dotted here and there with lifeless lagoons of brine that speck the sordid moonscape like craters of an undrinkable extra-terrestrial soup.

And that's not the sum-total of Pakistan's water troubles. In the pleasant, soft warmth of a golden early-summer's evening I find myself being led down, at last, to the banks of the river Indus to see and touch the life-giving water for myself. By the time it reaches this far south the river has already been diverted and somewhat polluted – enough to kill off the Indus river dolphin, and I certainly shouldn't choose to quench my thirst with this water. But it remains the well-spring of all life in Pakistan, fed by another melting glacier high up in the Himalayas. Perversely, in their greed for more water, some even suggested burning coal atop the glacier to speed up the process. Although this proposal has thankfully not been implemented, the glacier's usual cycle of melting and regrowth is nonetheless under threat from climate change, and its disappearance would mean disaster for Pakistan.

Tied into all these water issues, I realise, is the recurring inability of humanity to transcend the present moment. By looking to the past, Imperial and Pakistani governments could have seen the spectre of salination foreshadowed in the collapse of the great Indus Civilisation nearly four thousand years ago, a victim of its own extraordinary irrigation technology. If only the world could look to the future, we would see our own climate doom in the needless waste of today's materialistic lusts. And there is no better place to witness the emergence of this dangerous duality of short-sightedness than across the border, in India.

'Subcontinent' is a good word to describe the Indian peninsula, a land almost as varied in climate as any continent. While the south-west is deluged by up to eleven metres of rainfall per year, in the north some parts receive barely ten centimetres. The common culture that still pervades much of this country is a tradition with water at its heart. Through centuries of flood and drought Hindus especially have venerated India's rivers, but only since colonial times has man actively sought to control them. The coming decades could see the revival of a great proposal of characteristically reckless nineteenth-century ambition to join together the rivers of North and South India in a 'River Link Project', aiming to water dry Rajasthan. Rather than venerating the powers of nature, the project's advocates seek to 'dethrone the Monsoon', stripping it of its power to impose a geographical water inequality on the country. Entering the dry north before its brief rains arrive to cast their spell of green vibrancy on the parched Earth, I can see the origins of this temptation.

I am travelling on the famous Lahore-Delhi bus, the 'Call of the Frontier' instituted in 1999 to increase accord between two uneasy neighbours. It's an eight-hour drive to the Indian capital. Stepping off the bus in Delhi, I find it difficult to breathe. This has been called the most polluted city on the planet, any remaining greenery hidden beneath a heavy toxic smog. There are more than ten thousand people per square kilometre here, a city of seventeen million, and they soon demonstrate that the true water inequality in India is not geographical but social. While the wealthiest gobble up as much water in a day as the average European city-dweller uses in a month, the squalid lower classes queue for measly morsels at communal pumps. Even the lower-paid amongst the middle classes, dressed to impress in their clean business suits, betray their true, lowly status by standing in line. The rancid heart of this new India, descending in a smog of pollution, climate change and rampant inequality, is neither the river blue nor the forest green of the civilisation it is slowly choking, but black – coal black, as I shall soon witness for myself.

## 8: Decline and Fall

The Monsoon breaks like a sudden breath of sweet, fresh air after a long asphyxiation. Across the dry, sun-seared northern states of India reverberates a wave of joyful exhilaration: the long-awaited water has at last arrived; the tension that has tightened over weeks and months is shattered in an instant as life-giving liquor rains down from the heavens. The fragrance of the first fresh drops of water on the parched-dry ground erupts in an all-surrounding sweetness like nothing else on Earth. I can see the jubilation on the smiling face of the farmer who stands beside me, happy that his carefully cultivated crops can now start to soak up the elixir of life and grow. But it's a happiness mingled with relief: the same medley of emotions that must have met in the grateful minds of many million Indian farmers down countless generations every year the essential rains arrived. It's obvious, now, why this once mighty civilisation so worshiped the rain and rivers. If the rains failed, famine was the inevitable result. And it's the memory and fear of famine that still haunts the country's farmlands today.

My experience on this one small farm is, nowadays, an exception. It's one of just handful that have reverted to organic agriculture in a district dominated by more modern industrial methods. The living soil I can smell is rare, now, where the ground has mostly descended into dead, artificial dirt. This is no place of prosperity for nature or for man. For the great civilisation of India fell long ago, as did the exploitative

117

British Empire that followed it, and now the country struggles in the sticky mire that has followed their dual decline, a half-way industrialised chaos that can be the worst of both worlds. Over the past few decades, a programme of intense industrialisation has transformed the Punjab into a reliable breadbasket, ending the spectre of famine and making the country superficially self-sufficient in food.

But beneath this hides a growing reliance on imports of fuel, fertiliser and pesticides, and, ironically, even in its desperation to reassert a proud independence, India has rejected the philosophy of its pre-colonial heritage and copied the intensive farming practices of the capitalist West. The population has tripled since independence; one in five humans today is Indian. Yet the 'Green Revolution' that has facilitated this boom, whilst immensely profitable for multinational machinery and chemicals manufacturers, hasn't made for a better life for the majority. Three fifths now lack access to clean water, and the countryside is crumbling into ecological catastrophe.

What's more, the high yields brought about through industrial farming can't be sustained indefinitely. 'Fighting against Nature,' my host observes, presciently, 'it's a fight we cannot win'. Pests are defiantly evolving resistance to pesticides; soil stripped of its ecosystems and raped of its nutrients can no longer sustain high yields without the pouring on of more and more fertiliser. Stories abound of farmers driven into debt-induced suicide by the rising costs of chemicals and genetically-modified seeds. Promised prosperity through this new way of working but finding only poverty, perhaps a quarter of a million smallholders in the last two decades have found life too difficult to bear. More deaths, cancers and birth defects come directly from the chemicals, with sixty-seven widely-banned substances still used liberally on Indian farms. Poor labelling, widespread illiteracy and sheer desperation to bolster shrinking yields have led to a rampant over-use of these 'magic' quick-fix solutions that manufacturers and distributors have done little to stop. So, as the population rises still further, will Indian agriculture's long-term unsustainability doom the country to a decline of deeper devastation than anything seen before?

Not necessarily. My friend is one of a vanguard of newly organic farmers exhibiting a renewed reverence for nature, melding together the best of modern expertise with traditional, natural techniques to get reliable yields out of healthy ground. The crops I'm looking at are local varieties, adapted to this environment and requiring only Jeevamruta feed – a boiled-down mixture of herbs and dung. A swooping swallow – now a rare sight on India's farmlands – whirls across my vision, telling of a rejuvenated ecosystem, where pest-easting spiders and pollinators thrive once again. Organic farming is harder work, of course. It flies in the face of advice from most Indian agriculturalists – and the multinationals – who argue that there are too many people on the small-holder farms that dominate Indian agriculture; that computers and machinery should displace labourers who would be better-off crowding into the cities in search of modern, indoor jobs. The organic narrative turns this on its head: couldn't the country's swelling numbers be counted as a blessing, a new organic workforce doing real jobs alongside Nature?

It's cause for hope. But as I hobble eastwards in the humid heat of a rickety train, I'm soon reminded that none of this will save India from a deeper plight. Outside, the wide open landscape glistens in its painted coat rain. Not so long ago, the vast skies above it were host to forty million vultures. But the air is empty now, the magnificent birds become victims of poisonous painkillers that lately laced the carcasses of livestock on which they feasted. As we enter Jurkhand province, a new cloud takes their place on the horizon: one that bodes of a still-darker disaster that could bring about the fall of all forms of life we know and love.

I've come to visit the unquenchable fires of Jharia, one of the great coal-mining states of India. First set off more than a century ago, here baking seams of coal continuously burn, their flames fanned still fiercer year on year by the escalating extraction of this filthy fuel. Nowhere more deserves the title 'Hell on Earth'. I stand now on the precipice of a vast mine, tearful and terrified at what we have done.

On one side of me stretches mile after mile of piled-up black bile, mountains of dead organic remains disgorged from their million-year resting place to feed humanity's growing greed for electricity, the deadly drug to which we're now hopelessly addicted. On the other side Earth

120

gives way to a gargantuan man-made chasm – forest, field and flora obliterated to leave a lifeless pit, save for the scuttling, wheezing miners and scavengers who cough up lungs of black dust.

Surely, this is Hell indeed. Except that these pour souls suffer not for their own but for someone else's sins. Here, then, have I found, at last, the black heart of humanity's transgression. A world of unimaginable beauty, hacked, burned and blasted into a wasteland by crushed and broken slaves. And what for? 'Development'. 'Progress'. 'Luxury' for their demonic masters, and greed for more – more of what? What can possibly justify this sacrilege of suffering? These transient trinkets and comforts we greedily consume? Things that will themselves be dust in a decade, century, millennium. Solely for this pittance have we sold our paradise. And what will become of humanity, with all its love and life and creativity? Ruined and forgotten, by our own short-term selfishness we too will be destroyed. From Eden to Oblivion: hark how the 'mighty' fall!

# 9: Cycles
## *Through China*

A wide and enticing country brews, always, just beyond our western comprehension, like a cauldron of constant change the taste of whose broth we never can be sure. Such is the allure of tantalising China: a rich civilisation veiled behind a mist of mystery. And I, like so many awe-stricken adventurers, am drawn irresistibly thence. There is only one open border between India and China. Fortunately, this lies on the wild fringes of the scarcely-populated Sikkim province, an oasis of natural beauty abounding with such fauna as leopard, bear, deer, wolf, badger and golden eagles severely threatened elsewhere. Trekking slowly up into the four kilometre high Nathu La mountain pass, a portion of the ages-old Silk Road until recently barred to non-Indian nationals, I watch one whirl above me. Lulled by the loveliness of this sun-splashed spectacle of beauty – the abounding blue of the cloud-streaked sky, the vivacious verdancy of the forest, the perfect ice white and soft slate grey of the reclining mountains – it's almost as if I've stepped out of time and trouble. Hours ease by unmarked in my gentle amble, and I cross into Tibet with an overwhelming sense of awe and peace.

But trouble survives, if latent, even here, a soil stained by the blood of many in the brutal clash between Chinese officials and Tibetan separatists for control of this cherished plateau. My many mountain-dwelling days, coloured by the rich experience of ancient

Buddhist rituals still playing out in those high hills, could not shield me from the grim reality awaiting further down. The regional capital Lhansa, a 'development zone' growing with the same rapidity as so many Chinese settlements hastening to 'westernise' themselves, is where I again meet modernity. It is with some regret that I board the world's highest railway, though I turn down its offer of a direct forty-hour bullet to Beijing, preferring to make my way north and eastwards piece by piece. The journey, set against a backdrop of sweeping Chinese scenery, is not an unpleasant one. There's change afoot at every stop, it's true. But there's also an ancient Chinese way and wisdom at the heart of these scattered communities that refuses to be conquered despite Maoist and then Capitalist assaults. The cherry trees still blossom in the fertile valleys; the temple bells still ring from the hills. The words of Confucius still resound, if you listen for them – words about harmony with nature and with one another that the central government would do well to hear.

It used to be said that Beijing was a city of nine million bicycles, until the choking smog of coal fires and cars made cycling here toxic. In 2018, I find the air cleaner, with many of those fires and vehicles replaced by more efficient electric alternatives, though I don't quite bring myself to cycle those congested, still-polluted streets. Slowly, the smoke is clearing, it seems: industrialisation doesn't have to accompany growing prosperity; the bicycles need not bow out to cars. A fresh wind of change is blowing here, buoyed on by a unique Chinese optimism and a government that at least cares about climate change and the environment – or does it?

In a brand new electric car, I'm zipped northwards on the highway to Inner Mongolia by the local environmental campaigner who became my friend and guide. In recent years the Chinese have pioneered better, longer-lasting batteries that mean we can travel two hundred miles between stops to charge. These twenty- to thirty-minute breaks, familiar to electric car users the world over, give us chance to pause and watch the world go by, or to walk, escaping the faceless grey blot of each filling station car park to explore the surrounding countryside as we discuss the future of his country and its 'green' industry. It's very likely, he explains, that the power charging our car will come from a new suite of renewable generators springing up across China as it strides ahead to develop more efficient wind and solar generators and, in embarrassingly stark contrast to its neighbour India and the supposedly enlightened Germany, phases out dirty coal.

But this isn't coming without costs of its own. The government has displayed little democratic concern when it comes to pushing through its renewables revolution whatever the social and – ironically – environmental costs. New hydroelectric dams throttle and flood ancient rivers and valleys, and wind and solar's slates are far from clean. Could the 'greening' of the dragon be more about political power and so-called 'greenwash' in the eyes of the world than a genuine commitment to the well-being of China's inhabitants? Alas, our destination suggests this may be so.

Baotou is the world's largest source of rare Earth elements – the very precious metals on which a growing glut of mobile telephones, computers, solar panels, wind turbines and, yes, even our electric cars' batteries – depend. China prides itself on providing more than ninety-five per cent of the global supply. And as the world stampedes towards renewables and the batteries needed to make up for their intermittency, its economic leverage can only increase. But those mining these metals, and their neighbours, see few of the benefits. In the decade to 2012, the population of this town plummeted ten-fold to just three hundred, and it's not difficult to see why its people fled. The once fertile farmland has been poisoned by sulphuric acid and solvents released during metal extraction; livestock has died, and crops are laced with toxins. Putrid ponds of waste fester, so laced with expensive elements that residents were prosecuted for trying to sell samples.

Our greed for more precious metals is ripping ever deeper scars into our planet. All because we seek to prop up unsustainable levels of electricity consumption through 'renewable' ways of producing it and fail to recycle what we've already used in all the gadgets – such gleaming gems of human innovation – that we thoughtlessly toss away and replace. Electric cars and solar panels are, at present, little better than gimmicks, designed to keep us consuming and living fast-paced lives while fooling ourselves that we're free from environmental sin. At least the Chinese urban poor will stop complaining that their cities are too polluted to breathe in, even if that pollution is merely swept out of sight elsewhere.

On my way to Beijing I passed through Wen'an in Hebei, famed for its forests, streams and wildlife until the world's greed for guilt-free plastic brought the recycling industry here. Nothing green survived in the resulting dead zone, where factories pumped the fumes of burnt unrecyclable remnants into the plasticised lungs of the stressed inhabitants. The industry was shut down in 2011, but China continues to produce and import vast quantities of plastics, and my host assures me that the same problems are resurfacing elsewhere. They call it modernisation. 'We used to fear water-borne diseases,' he tells me. 'But the land was healthy. Now these diseases are gone, but people get high blood pressure from the stress, or cancer from the plastics.' The deadly cycle of poverty still wheels on.

## 10: Judgement
*From China to Korea*

Somewhere beneath the steel spires of China's biggest city lie buried the remnants of a tiny village of ages past. Somewhere – overridden by congested roads and railways, over-trodden by millions of trapesing feet – lie the bones of countless generations now forgotten. It seems ironic that even in a city where the majority claim to adhere to the traditional religious beliefs including ancestor-worship, pictures of the past should be so utterly obliterated. Modern generations have traded the rolling landscape of their forebears for yet another shrine to capitalist modernity, with towers reaching for the heavens as if to proclaim the greatness of mankind's tall triumph over his small beginnings.

Do they look down in judgement on their children, those deceased whose every cherished custom has been cast off, whose every landmark of their lives has been dismantled? Will future generations judge it a swap well made, when they look upon the splendour – or the ruin – of Shanghai? But theirs is not the power to prevent or to protest; the dreamed-up and the dead dwell, alike, in silence, looking on while the living labour, love and lust and do what they believe is bes, oblivious.

Shanghai has little time to stop and ponder; this is a city of fast-paced production and consumption, a busy-ness that chokes the very air and smothers the mind in a thoughtless smog, while wheels wear down and chimneys churn their pointless plumes of smoke. Ferried across a choppy sea to Seoul, I almost feel as though I haven't moved at all, so similar appears the Korean capital. A high-speed train has raced me from the port to the city, a fireworks display of garish lights and screens at this bustling evening hour. Aboard the city's busy subway, I find myself surrounded by a distracted population that seems to be somewhere entirely different, lost in the dream-worlds of their telephone screens. Almost every ear is plugged. This is the world's most wired-up, switched-on city, drowning out both day and night with synthesised sound and light. It's almost as if the people here are afraid of the dark, afraid of the silence.

Ninety per cent of South Korea's population is huddled into cities; nearly half of its fifty-million-strong population in Seoul alone. Amidst this crowd I stand out conspicuously: nearly everyone around me is of Korean ethnicity. But even more so than the inhabitants of Shanghai, these have adopted a conspicuously non-native way of life. This country pioneered high-speed internet, in 2005, when ninety-seven per cent of the populace was already plugged into internet-connected 'smart 'phones'. The boon of universal healthcare jostles against the modern phenomenon of low birth rates to create a rapidly ageing, albeit well-educated, society more reminiscent of modern-day Europe than most of Asia, its neighbour Japan excepted. The country has been praised, in recent decades, for adopting 'Western'-

style democracy and for a religious tolerance unparalleled in this turbulent region.

This is also the home of the movement for a capitalist solution to climate change. It's with a sad sigh that I look upon the headquarters of the 'Green Climate Fund' and the 'Green Growth Institute', those vocative advocates of the notion that companies and governments can still make money – still 'develop' into capitalist copies of the West – whilst fighting climate change. Everything I've seen on my journey so far has left me in little doubt that they are mistaken. Capitalism causes over-consumption, which causes climate change. The one cannot be detached from the other.

But there's little sign of this notion in Korea. All around me flash signs bearing familiar names – 'Hyundai', 'Samsung', 'LG'. The architecture is a mish-mash of steel and glass rising out of the traces of older, rather different flavours of design. It's a city forged through decades' worth of destruction and reconstruction, a city that races ahead of the game and doesn't let the past linger for long. From the perspective of capitalist growth and material 'progress', I find myself in a boom town: being at the cutting edge of technology is, surely, modern-day South Korea's biggest preoccupation.

Or is it? It's not all smiles that I see in Seoul. The English homonym seems expressly inapt, for this is the city where 'soul' seems most lacking. The supposed tolerance of the government stops short at conscientious objection, and the arrest of Jehovah's Witnesses judged to be criminals for their pacifist objections to compulsory military service is a stark reminder of what people here are truly worrying about. The government spends fifteen per cent of its budget on the military; the spectre of its northern neighbour looms large. In its very desperation to be plugged in, taken away somewhere else – in its very denial of Korean culture and embrace of an entirely alien capitalistic emphasis on growth, technology and consumption – the South displays an urgency to distract itself from the ugly sister that cuts it off from mainland Asia, a monstrosity moulded from modernity's most devastating industrial war and now armed with technology's most terrifyingly destructive development, the atom bomb. Do the people of Seoul really want this Westernisation-on-steroids? Or are they simply afraid to be Korean, because they are afraid of what other Koreans might do?

Stepping outside the neon city, however, I find South Korea proper to be a quite different experience. Three-quarters of this country is mountainous, and the view from the train that zips me across the rugged ridges is quite as breath-taking as any I have seen elsewhere. It's Monsoon season, and down in the plains the air is hot and humid, but the picturesque province of Gyeongsang is at its most luscious. I've come to visit just three of the twelve World Heritage Sites that attract visitors to this peninsula, and here, at last, I find signs of the real Korea – remembrances of a lost past. Ruined temples and palaces and almost Pompeii-like preserved historical villages arouse deep feelings of connection with those who ruled, who lived, who worshipped here hundreds of years ago.

At the 2018 PyeongChang Winter Olympics (it had to be spelt with a capital 'C' to prevent any unfortunate confusion with the North Korean capital Pyeongyang) it wasn't the superficial glitz of digital technology that took centre stage in the opening ceremony. Instead, displayed on the digital screens were images of these: these sites of genuine heritage, these relics of an ancient splendour, and the forests and wetlands amidst which they nestle. In the late twentieth century, those areas were eroded without thought in the name of 'progress'. Now they are protected by no fewer than twenty National Parks in a country little larger than Scotland. Traditional Korean culture and architecture celebrated and encouraged harmony with nature. After decades of fear and distraction, we can hope, at least, that Korea might be at last reawakening to its true self. Yet still the shadow of the nuclear-armed North obscures the light of day.

## 11: Rubbish
*Across the Pacific*

I'm going in search of an island. It's no ordinary island. You won't find it on any map; it can't be seen from space. Yet it's the size of Texas. The only way to reach it is by sea, but you won't see it coming. You'll only know you've reached it when it already surrounds you. This is an aethereal island, one that didn't exist a century ago. An island composed of spent dreams and ugly remnants: the refuse of the twentieth and twenty-first centuries, the flotsam and jetsam of the wreckage of the modern world. A whirlpool of waste; a giant reef of rubbish.

Getting there, it's going to be a long journey – that I know for certain. The 'Great Pacific Garbage Patch', as my destination has come to be known since its not entirely unexpected discovery by a trans-Pacific sailor in 1999, lies at the nucleus of a swirling gyre of congregating ocean currents in the vast open ocean between Hawaii and Japan, which drags debris of all kinds from the coasts of Asia and North America into its poisoned plastic heart. Not many boats cross these waters – nearly four thousand miles separate the two archipelagos – and given that the huge tourist ocean liners that occasionally make the crossing are scarcely less harmful to the environment than aeroplanes, I'm seeking out a smaller ship that will take even longer than usual to traverse the distance. In 2008, a Japanese sailor managed this task on a boat powered entirely by waves.

The journey lasted nearly one hundred days, but without any greenhouse gas emissions at all.

My slow travel across the Pacific will be slightly faster, but by the slightly murkier means of a new solar- and sail-powered ship. When the sun shines and the wind blows, these renewable resources will replace our dirty diesel generator to propel us across the waves. I've crossed from Korea to Japan, that other Asian centre of innovation, to join a fishing expedition with a difference, trawling for trash rather than trout from the deeps. It's another irony to me that Japan, this crucible of science and research, this somewhat socialist society apparently content with economic stability rather than groping for growth, and the proponent and progenitor of rubbish-raking renewable transport, has facilitated and encouraged the production of so much of the cast-off clutter we're trying to collect.

Where have all those billions of gadgets – from computers to cameras, 'Walkmans' to wireless telephones – that Japanese companies have created and Japanese factories have proudly forged for half a century ended up? How much needless electronic waste has been piled up on land and at sea in the drive to produce ever smaller, faster, 'better' devices and simply throw away and replace their perfectly workable but redundant predecessors? So many amazing feats of technology, taken for granted then tossed away.

Shanghai, Seoul, Tokyo – all look the same to me, despite their respective countries' very different histories, cultures and social systems. All of them have been colonised by a capitalist consumerism alien to their surroundings in space and time. It's these putrid palaces of human pride that best epitomise the out-with-the-old culture that is ravishing our world's resources and plasticising our own environment.

It's a magical morning when I board the boat. With a gleaming sun and a healthy wind we're set for a sustainable start to our voyage. Yet there's no denying that I go with dread and fear. Ahead of us spans a stupefying stretch of swirling sea; once we're hundreds of miles from shore, there'll be no turning back. And watching the enchanting islands of Japan receding into the distance, a land-lover like myself cannot help but foster pangs of regret. Alas, the thoughts I flounder to find to distract myself from the long voyage ahead are far from comforting. Though this ocean flaunts serenity today, peering into its silvery ripples I can't avoid musing on the wild waves that whipped up these waters into a force of such destruction that fateful March day in 2011. And who knows what noxious nuclear nasties now lurk beneath the surface, the remnants of a toxic soup concocted in that nightmare collision between the sloshing sea and an ill-prepared nuclear power station?

Not all human waste is visible, and it's what can't be seen that has the most frightful effects. Invisible particulates that line our lungs are the cruellest consequence of city air pollution; radiation poisoning may only make itself known days, weeks or years after exposure, in painful, grisly ways. Think of poor Marie Curie, who became so radioactive the cookery books she merely touched are still too dangerous to handle today. When at long last we reach our island of rubbish, it becomes clear that the same is true here. There are a few larger items bobbing here and there – fishing nets that can catch and kill passing marine mammals, though there's nobody here to haul them in; bottle-top buoys and trashed toys flushed from rivers and beaches and swept out to sea. But most plastics soon disintegrate under the triple assault of salty spray, searing sun and unseen microorganisms, breaking into smaller and smaller pieces and leeching toxins into the blue.

So it is that we're surrounded by mostly unidentifiable remnants suffusing the surface, and hence the analogy of the semi-submerged island. It's difficult to believe just how vast this agglomeration is – mile after mile, hour after hour we plough our way through, picking up what pieces we can with a specially-designed scoop. But what we gather is all too literally a mere drop in the ocean. In fact, the most worrying thing of all is that the garbage patch isn't visible growing any bigger, even as the industrialised world pumps out more and more waste. All that rubbish must be going somewhere, but we can't see it.

Now we think we know the dirty truth. The pieces are becoming so small that they form an invisible plastic plankton, outnumbering real plankton in some parts of the ocean. These toxic trinkets are swallowed by plankton-eating fish, and slowly make their way up the food-chain. Pictures of sea-birds whose stomachs are stopped by indigestible pieces of their poisonous plastic

135

feasts are the most horrifyingly visible evidence of the damage done by marine pollution. But the plastics and heavy metals that we dump may be wreaking still greater damage in a more insidious form, and if you eat fish they're probably already infiltrating your own dinner-plate.

Flushing away our needlessly-produced, deadly toxic rubbish 'out of sight, out of mind' is really just another way in which humanity is slowly undermining our own survival. Again I stare down into the murky water, this time thinking of the dumped crates of computers, wrecked ships and scuttled nuclear submarines that reportedly line the ocean floor, rotting away. When will the unseen sludge oozing from this detritus begin to seep all too unstoppably into our lives? Will these spectres from a careless past come back to haunt humanity's future? Or can we clean up our societies and clear up the time-capsules of calamity we've already planted before it's too late? I fear that only time will tell.

## 12: Goodbye
*On Hawaii*

In the midst of the unimaginably vast, empty expanse that is the surface of the Pacific Ocean – the thin, glittering film across which we have slid for nearly a month – the first, precious sighting of land feels like the fulfilment of one's every hope and dream. For days I have feared that I would never reach this moment: that memories of solid Earth were nothing but the fantasies of a deluded mind, or worse that time would play some cruel trick upon us, standing still, so that every day we'd be doomed to relive the 'last' day again and again on this unbroken sea for all eternity, supposedly close to our conclusion but never actually reaching the end.

But my groundless fears were vanquished by that gratifying vision: a tiny spec growing, undeniably, hour by hour. We would not be lost, tossed on endless unnavigable waves: as soon as we saw that sumptuous sight we knew that we'd be saved. I simply stood and stared for many minutes, at my heart's content just to see undeniable land. No longer did I will the wishful hours away; no longer did I mind, were it to take a day or week or another month to reach it. All that mattered was that land was assured, and that one day we'd be home.

Never had I thought to greet so gratefully the shores of Hawaii, a life-saving outpost in the midst of the sea. As we disembarked, stumbling on my shaky sea-legs I almost felt like tumbling down and kissing the very ground. I grasped for a handful of dirt; to me it felt like gold-dust, and the sound of waves on rocks, of birds, of crowds of people was like all the music I'd ever want to hear. It's places like this, after a long, slow, landless voyage, that make one appreciate how, on an Earth three-quarters covered by water, just how precious and exceptional is solid ground. Hawaii is unusual in that here the ground is growing, welling up in an effusive eruption from Earth's secret heart. The first thing that I want to do is to explore the remaining idylls of these islands, to see the hope-inspiring symbol of new natural creation for myself – a perfect antidote to the artificial archipelago of waste I've just witnessed.

Hawaii is much larger that I'd imagined it. The northernmost group of islands in Polynesia, it is spread across one and a half thousand miles, with a human population of one and a half million. It was annexed to the USA as long ago as 1898, and around me I see the usual signs of imported American culture: cars, roads, shopping centres, fast food, obesity – the ugly faces of capitalism are a recent plague on this once pristine place. But there's also an astounding amount of surviving natural beauty, as I'm about to discover. The erupting volcano of Kilauea is in the Volcanoes National Park in the south of 'Big Island', and it's not difficult to find somebody to lead me there. But on my way there's a stop I simply can't miss making, and quite by chance I come upon the perfect guide.

This man isn't from Hawaii. He's from Tuvalu, half way to Australia. But now he works as a tour guide, trying to raise awareness for his homeland's plight at the same time as earning a living. For Hawaii is truly unusual in its continual growth; ten million years ago this was open ocean. Elsewhere in the Pacific, the trend is almost entirely the other way: in perhaps only a hundred years, Tuvalu will be gone, swallowed by the sea. And the clinching evidence to pin down the culprit of this sudden catastrophe is on display right here, at the Mauna Loa observatory on top of the world's most massive volcano.

It wasn't for nothing that Charles Keeling chose this site to begin making his measurements of carbon dioxide in 1958. High above most of the murk emitted by mankind, the air is clear and well-mixed by fresh westerly winds. We've had to come most of the way by car, but are able to make the final ascent by foot, spurning the slick road for a rockier ascent. It's a beautiful sight before us, gleaming atop the mountain: the place that proved that humble humanity does have the power to change the planet, and pinned the blame for climate change squarely on us. Somewhere swirling around this mountain, I think guiltily as we gaze, those fumes our car has just disgorged are making a slight but not inconsequential contribution to the climbing concentration of carbon dioxide, a trend Keeling noticed with horror and which for more than sixty years we've continually failed to check. The air even here isn't so pristine as it might look, after all. That's the terrifying truth that he found. And in a chaotic system such as our atmosphere, even single particle of invisible pollutant can have profound effects.

As we journey on towards Kilauea, my companion tells me more about the plight of the millions most undeniably affected by climate change because of the needless greed of others far away. The island atolls – Pacific paradises inhabited for millennia – are drowning alarmingly quickly. Tuvalu has already lost one of its islands, and every year the sea encroaches a little further, like a lengthening shadow before the setting of the sun. The losses are catalysed by deteriorating reefs and inadequate conservation measures, but there can be no denying the major driving factor: global sea-level rise. Water expands when it warms; melting glaciers over land leek millions of litres into the oceans every day. The combined effect could be a death-knell, and not just for Tuvalu. The twenty-nine atolls of the Marshall islands are just six feet on average above sea level; their inhabitants are already reduced to creating their own islands of rubbish, shoring their land up with trash to hold back the tide. The Maldives are even lower. Nowadays, the stormy season brings such severe floods that their thousands of inhabitants are forced to flee their homes. And sea-level rise is slow to start but hard to halt; this is just the beginning. Even if the world's emissions stopped today the ocean's encroachment might continue for a century. Soon, there'll be no higher ground to which to flee.

We drive on through the fertile forest of Hawaii, marvelling at the multitude of life thriving on its rich volcanic soils. All these birds and flowers, some unique to this island, must have had hardy ancestors that braved the winds and seas to colonise this remote corner. But once established, life clings on, even in the harshest of environments. It will survive, whatever we do, in some form or another, to flourish again in a future aeon. But as my guide and I reach an abrupt halt where the road suddenly stops, buried beneath a wall of magma that erupted several years ago now, I ponder. This century could well be the final farewell for Pacific islanders, as well as for many of the species that call our planet home. My path has blocked; I can go no further. Has humanity, too, reached the end of the road? Is it time, my friends, to say 'goodbye'?

End of Section 1

## 13: Renewal
### *Reflecting from the Future*

Forgive me if I begin at the end. For the end is near, now: I can feel it in my bones. These my eyes, which looked upon so many of the world's ancient wonders, have grown dim – like those wonders themselves, which one by one went out, melting like stars before the morning sun into a hazy dream. There is only one wonder left for me to look upon: the dizzy light through a whitewashed sky as a few birds circle the scrubby hills; life clinging on. And it is a wonder indeed that it does cling on, after all that has befallen. Here, where I began a hundred tumultuous years ago, will I end.

I sit and watch these hills every day now, trying to accustom myself to the changed landscape that surrounds me, trying to call it 'beautiful'. But there is little left of custom or continuity these days: change, wicked and unyielding change, is the only constant, year by year. Of course, you will say that we still have the cycle of the seasons, the lengthening and shortening of days, which even mankind cannot touch until we find a way to move the very Earth in its orbit. But these 'seasons' as you call them now are not the seasons I once knew. The trees, you know, used to shed their leaves for the winter. The colours – oh, what colours did I see, in the amber autumns of my youth! Here there was an orchard then, and apples grew – huge, rosy apples – in the open air. The damson trees hung heavy with fruit as their leaves mellowed from the richest summer green into a gorgeous yellow. The forest floor became an orange carpet, and the hedgerows wore garlands of bright red berries, matched for colour only by the dying displays of sycamore and maple. The blackberries alone, now, have survived, where the trees and hedges and the beauty of the autumn's dying fire have gone. Oh, how I would love to wonder again in the forests of my younger days!

Some of the birds used to fly south in the winter, to avoid the bitter cold. In those days the temperature would fall below the freezing point of water even here, and not just once or twice but for several days or weeks in a year. And there was snow, from time to time – a white blanket! It was already less common than it had been, even when I was young, for the signs of change were already becoming visible. I don't remember when I last saw snow. Perhaps it was when I travelled to the Arctic Circle, before it became all ocean. But that was more than forty years ago! It is an antiquated word now, 'snow'. When it melted in the spring, that was when the world really came alive: then there was a chorus of birds! Not like this cackle you get now. No, then the birds used to sing! The dawn chorus would come as a magic melody of voices to rouse us from our sleep – if we were prepared to listen. I wish I had listened more often, when I had the chance. But there was such a din of distractions that used to fill our lives then. Now our lives are quiet and empty, yet though I sit all day with my ears open, there aren't any songs to hear.

But summer's coming now. It will be my last, I know it. My aged frame cannot cope with another round of searing heat. And perhaps I can't bear it, anyway, to see the ground so parched and perished – not again. To think that August was once my favourite time of year! I used to go out walking and exploring – yes, even in August! – to see nature in all its fullest, freshest vitality. Of course, back then a day above thirty degrees was a rarity. It was warm, comfortably warm – not hot, even outside. Not scorching. I don't recall when it first passed forty degrees. I don't recall the last August day that failed to reach thirty. Perhaps '84 had one or two. They say it was a cool year. To me they all muddle into one, these days.

But not so in my youth: I remember those distinct, delicious days still clearly. I remember cool summer breezes and winter nights by the fire to keep warm. I remember daffodils in February and carpets of bluebells in April. I remember big orange pumpkins and squashes in October, and nippy November 'bonfire nights' – and how they used to bet on it snowing at Christmas! And I remember the warnings, the slow realisation that things were changing, the sceptics that claimed it wasn't! You wouldn't believe it now, but it's true, there were sceptics who said the whole thing wasn't real! It must have been thirty years from when they first noticed, before I was even born, that mankind was changing the planet, before at last the world's leaders were convinced.

And we thought, then, that we'd caught it in time, that we could prevent it. I was young and enthusiastic; I hadn't seen what I've seen now. We thought it wouldn't happen, that we'd change our society in time, instead of changing the climate. But of course, you know that it was too late. We didn't know our paradise was disappearing until it was already almost lost. The war got in the way, of course, and in the end we just couldn't give them up, those luxuries to which we'd become so quickly accustomed. We couldn't cut the emissions fast enough after all. And so this, I'm afraid, is what we're left with. We lost all those luxuries anyway, in the end. And so many people too, in the famine and flooding – how many of us are there now? Nobody knows. That's the war for you – the war in the south that never stops. Nobody knows anything much about the rest of the world, do they, any more?

I did, once. When I was still young and naive, and genuinely scared by the prophesies of climate doom, I set out one day – in the spring of 2018 – to see the world, and the worrying signs of how we were destroying it, for myself. 'Slow Travel', I called it, but it was really just travel, as we would know it today: in fact, you might call it fast. For not only by foot did I go, but also by bus and train and boat, when such things were still used. Only I'd stop at every place I passed through, to drink in each culture and to know each unique people, if briefly, that still just about survived back then. I saw London and Paris, Greece before the war destroyed it, Egypt and Saudi Arabia before they were subsumed into the Great Desert and became a wasteland. Iran, India, Bangladesh, Korea. These names mean nothing to you now; then they were great and populous countries. And I went across the wide Pacific Ocean on a slow boat to the island of Hawaii. The Americas: that was where my eyes were truly opened, and my adventures really began.

## 14: Design
*Across Texas*

'Global warming? There ain't no such thing! Didn't y' hear? That's just a conspiracy cooked up by the Chinese. An' the leftists. You're a leftist, ain't ye? Now you listen to me, mister. You leave all that clap-trap out o' here. We're done with commies, we're done with Obama, now we're goanna take America back to bein' the great nation it once was, an' you can sling your hook if you dun' like it, 'cos we ain't lettin' nobody stand in our way.'

I was beginning to regret broaching the subject of climate change with this burly bartender, who, as he towered over me, looked somewhat more than my match. He must have a gun, I thought – everyone around here has a gun – and perhaps he wouldn't turn down the chance to chase me out of town with bullets at my heels, or worse. Certainly, I didn't fancy my chances in an old-style showdown. But then he just chuckled, and the other patrons – two well-built gentlemen who'd been quietly sipping sodas at the far end of the bar – chuckled with him. Evidently, they saw me more as a joke than a threat. 'You got yourself a crazy one there, Bill,' said one. 'I'd keep your crazy ideas to yourself, if I were you,' he laughed. 'No-one's listenin', anyhow.'

How right he was, in this latter observation. At least the idea of climate change had reached here, I thought, grasping for consolation – even into the middle of the oil belt. But, for certain, nobody was listening. Though I was newly arrived in town, so much was

147

already clear. Outside on the river-wide, ruler-straight highway, thousands of petrol-powered wagons, each as big as five horses, proudly purred. Inside, the air-conditioning hissed and sighed, taking the heat of half a dozen diners chomping stakes almost too big to bite. This was not a place of abstinence or climate-conscious constraint.

I'd already seen the oil wells, relentlessly-churning and dotted across the desert like an insatiable swarm of mosquitos. But oil was not what frightened me in this dusty Texan town. That black gold was nothing more than liquid – mindless, formless, a trickling treacle flowing where it could regardless of what flowers of beauty were swallowed beneath its sickly stain. What frightened me was the heedless contentment of the people who so blithely pumped it out. This wasn't the America I'd seen in Hawaii, nor even that I'd arrived to on the parched Pacific coast. This wasn't the Texas of the great thinkers of enlightened science, who'd even launched men to the Moon. What I saw here was the most tangible example of a state of opinionated, anti-science stubbornness, suspicious of anything foreign in concept or in substance, that has sadly begun to slink across the whole industrialised world. A people that saw the grim reality of climatic change ahead, and simply laughed and turned its back. This was America in denial. This was the America of President Trump.

The clapped-out old bus that jolted me into the deepest South of this southerly state was shared with Texans of an entirely different sort to the well-off white males who'd given me such short shrift. Here, I met a pantheon of wonderful diversity only observable amidst the poorer classes in such a country built upon migration. We were composed of a spectrum of skin-colours and ethnicities; to my ears came a medley of American twang and Spanish scintillation, suffusing the hot air like an undulating undercurrent. But many of the passengers remained silent, staring out into the wide, dry landscape beyond the molten metal shimmer of this baking grey road. Texas was in the midst of another painful drought, the latest in a succession that has dogged this country, returning like a biting invasive insect that refuses to be brushed away, since the turn of the millennium.

This was the land where the devastating effects of human interference were made so chokingly clear in the dust-bowl years of the 1930s, when the conversion of great swathes of grassland to ploughed fields literally blew up in the farmers' faces. When the rains fell slack, the unprotected soil was stripped away by rust-red wind storms, leaving only desert. And yet despite Texas' deepening droughts it's a state still in denial: still the country's biggest beef producer; still the sixth-largest extractor of oil in the world when ranked alongside entire countries; still guzzling the fifth most energy per person in the United States, generating more electricity than the whole United Kingdom. They say 'everything is bigger in Texas'. From what I saw, everything – from waistlines to the rich list's wallets, from pollution to poverty – was still expanding.

But as we made our way down from the vast agricultural acreages and colossal colonies of corn-fed cattle belching out their planet-warming methane, and slipped into the lush landscape of the breath-taking Rio Grande River, I was abruptly reminded that there was one thing in Texas that certainly wasn't expanding any more, immigration. There, beyond the rippling waters of the wide water-course that carved its stunning cascade through this red, rocky region so many millennia ago, I saw for myself the modern-day enhancement of what was evidently not a punishing enough natural barrier – miles of desert and a magnificent but treacherous river – to deter travellers from the south. 'Trump's Wall'. A thousand miles of breachable, haphazard metal fencing that already scarred across America's rusty base in an attempt to plug the leaks, was now being replaced by a supposedly impenetrable span of solid concrete. Whether the billions of dollars required to complete it would ever be found I couldn't know, but already the finished sections had seen migration rates go the same way as America's climate change pledges and Texas' renewables industry. Migrant population levels were now as static as the blades on the Texan wind turbines that once supplied ten per cent of its electricity. But in time, of course, the cracks were bound to show.

Looking at the ugly structure ascending across this ruined paradise, it was clear that the president's promise that the wall would be 'beautiful' had turned out to be no more than a 'Donald Trump fact'. But the isolationism that the wall represents is sadly all too real.

Cutting itself off from the needs of its neighbours; responding to the calls of climate scientists and the needy poor by simply shouting louder until they can't be heard; carrying on regardless to churn out the gaseous effluent of its luridly lavish lifestyle while the rest of the world burns: Trump's America was trying with all its might to shut out the truth. But it was designing for itself a prison from which there could be no release.

## 15: Utopia
*From the United States to Cuba*

The heat of a long, lingering Louisiana summer simmered still as I made my slow way across the humid wetlands of that southerly state. It's a country of wide deltas and stretching coastal marshes, a buzzing frontier between the amazing lifeforms of land, sea and sky united in a swampy soup of vitality. Each day, roaming a little further along that blessed shore, I was dazzled by new sights of nature. Ibis and egrets, stilt-legged waders, flapped in beautiful display as they landed, while a daily drama of shifting shades played out across the vast stage of the limitless sky. What a crucible of creation this must have been, I mused, through the countless millennia when all this life teemed unseen by human eyes. What untold elation must have risen in the hearts of those who, following the river, first saw where the wide mouth of mighty Mississippi opens like a chest spilling its treasure into the ocean waves.

Looking upon these natural wonders, I'm not surprised so many ancient American tribes chose, long ago, to settle near these coasts. Nowadays, of course, though their descendants preserve, surprisingly well, their ancestral customs, their cherished paradise isn't quite so pure. European adventurers and their progeny have looked upon this striking sight with somewhat different eyes, and although along most of the coast Louisiana still gradually dissolves, as it always did, in a mushy marsh from land into sea, long stretches have been solidified by the less sublime machinations of modern-day man. Canals rip through the flatlands, bearing strong, salty seawater inland to quench the insatiable thirst of oil and gas extractors, damaging miles of formerly freshwater swamp along the way.

Avoiding the developed parts of the coast, I too turned at times inland, but even there the broad pine flatwood forests are losing ground to city sprawl, and another ecosystem is under threat. Conservation corridors brought in to link some species' dispersed strongholds are perhaps an indication of a people waking up to the need to protect its biological bounty, but it's been a long time coming. Perhaps it's the very vastness, the seeming boundlessness of America, where individual states are the size of my entire country, that fools people here into a false complacency about the limitless capacity of nature, as though whatever they do to the oceans, the wetlands, the wilderness they will still be there, continuing over the next horizon. Nature's display here is so bewilderingly big and beautiful that it's difficult to believe that man has the power to change it: a disbelief long since shaken off on smaller, more crowded isles.

But the danger we dabble with when we play too profligately with our relatively new-fangled fire was made all to evident here not so long before my visit, a danger that biological corridors will do little more to stymie than a sandbag on the seashore pitched against a rising tide. When at last I reached the tall American towers of bedraggled New Orleans, the spider at the heart of this web of human intervention, the calamity of Katrina could still be seen, especially in the east, with housing blocks left vacant and homeless left unhoused since 2005. The memory of that loss remains sour for many of the people that I meet. But what's still changing is the climate. The strong storms will become more common, and the habitat loss that accumulated, year by year, piece by piece, as the precious protective wetlands were built upon and drained, comes back to bite now when the weather's not so fair: when the levee breaks and there's nothing left to soften nature's blow.

Where, then, to escape this recurring theme of self-inflicted destruction? Is there no place where human society's harmony with its own habitat is maintained? I'd heard tell, long ago, of an island where things were done differently: a place so divorced from the American way of life that, though little more than a hundred miles away, the two countries were all but cut off for decades. But by the autumn of 2018, it had become possible to go to the island and explore it for myself: for the first time since the fifties, boats were running again from the fringes of Florida to the sunny, sandy coasts of Castro's Cuba.

No place I know of presents such a conundrum as Cuba. Its ramshackle houses, partly dilapidated, look like cold, concrete cast-offs from Cold War Eastern Europe, at first sight a throwback to that unenlightened dystopia of faux-socialist sham. And yet, I sensed at the same time a proud authenticity in those walls, an eager recognition that this was no globalised, 'developing' outpost of Anglo-American colonial capitalism: things were different here. The people I met were friendly and communicative, not at all like prisoners in a den of misery desperate to get out. They are exceptionally well-educated, well cared-for by a health service that produces more doctors per capita than anywhere else – which are, perhaps, Cuba's most treasured export. These people work for the state and share in its produce; they receive fair rations of food, and enjoy state-run television and wages that are low but equal and sufficient given that most services are free. Perhaps this is why loosening the travel embargo hadn't had a Berlin Wall effect here: the people didn't want to leave. They were, outwardly at least, happy. Could this really be the actualisation of the socialist dream?

But outward prosperity can mask darker realities, and this is not a land where dissenting views are aired to potentially loose-tongued tourists. If Cubans were so contented, I wondered, why would there have been a need to trap them on the island in the first place? When I ask a jovial market vendor, in my potholed Spanish, about the provenance of his produce, I learn that most of it probably followed me into port. 'From over the sea,' he tells me, but I'm not sure he knows what he means. In a country where eighty per cent of food is imported but hardly anyone has travelled abroad, something isn't right. So, eschewing the tourist-tailored shoreline façade, I venture down darkened streets and out beyond the town, until I come upon, inevitably, the barbed wire, the armed guards, the feeling I really shouldn't be here: the sure signs I've come upon the most infamous of Cuba's many, many prisons. It had to be, of course, that there were few dissenting voices, for any that were vocal once would have ended up in one of these places, alongside so many other political detainees. But the sight before me now is not one of Castro's creations, but rather America's single long-standing link with this its least favourite neighbour. I whisper its name with a shudder: Guantanamo Bay. The notorious base has been retained through all these decades, and, since 2002, has housed a prison as severe as any torturous Cuban cell. Torturous political repression is one thing the two governments evidently both hold to be essential. I've searched far and wide for a haven of free, sustainable socialism. On all three counts it seems, after all, that there is no such place.

## 16: Dusk
*From Cuba to Canada*

Entombed forever in a place where sunlight never shines. Beaten and broken by remorseless hands and feet. Tortured until I no longer recognise truth from falsehood. Consumed by fear, is there anything left of what I once was – anything left of myself? This was not my reality. But it was, I fear, somebody's reality. Over there, across the bay, but a wind's breath away, behind walls of secrecy that, but for a few hundred metres of precious space, would close me in too. It's a fragile gift, freedom. We seldom think how easily we might lose it. But if we become a threat or inconvenience to those numerous or powerful enough to take it away, take it they will. And who is there to stop them?

My musings were dark as I dreamed away a night beneath the lonely stars on the less shadowy side of Guantanamo Bay and waited for the grey light of the dawn. Seized as long ago as 1898, the American enclave is still regarded as illegal by Cuba. But what can it do against a power waxed so strong? What could the Taino people do when, four centuries before that, the Spaniards first arrived with their not-so-benign curiosity and their guns and their steel and started to demand gold? Perhaps this island really was, until then, like an Eden before the fall. The people, said Columbus, were 'gentle and laughing'; they 'do not murder or steal'. After joy turned to mourning, after gentility was met with the sword, after strange men from over the sea taught this childlike land the meaning of murder and took from it people, pasture, precious stones – whatever they could steal – is it any wonder that today's Cubans, like their dwindled, displaced forebears, should want to resist the interference of other peoples with other ideas of how things ought to be?

I spend many days on that fascinating island. In a place whose people once eagerly traded unesteemed gold for cheap Spanish brass, a metal of more mesmerising lustre whatever the world might say of its value, I found a people again placing pragmatic utility above symbols of status, defying the modern world's measures of 'success'. Yes, most of the food is imported, but what's grown here is nearly all organic, grown with pride and without fertilisers and pesticides. There are so few farm animals that to kill a cow without special permission is, as it should be, a heinous crime. The hunger seen under Spanish rule has been abolished by the provision of a basic ration to everyone. Nor is this well-educated people afraid to innovate: Genetic Modification of crops, stymied elsewhere, was already bringing benefits here, free from control by unscrupulous chemical multinationals with ulterior intensions.

There is the germ of something truly good on Cuba, I thought in the quiet twilight of my final full day there. If only the government's political paranoia was relaxed, and the people could speak freely, I'm sure they wouldn't have such very bad things to say. Maybe the free and happy spirit of the Taino still lingers in the soil,

158

where up to a million of these ancients once sustainably lived. Maybe one day, nourished by that spirit, the blossoms of paradise will bloom here once again.

English with a North American twang was never far from my earshot on the coral-white coasts of Cuba, but I soon learned that it seldom sprung from the mouths of its nearest neighbour the US. Whilst contact has been cold with its ideological and territorial rival, Cuba has had for Canada a long-standing softness. The Canadians bring both planeloads of tourists and bulky shiploads of lucrative trade. And it was on one of these boats that I managed to stow myself, with a little luck and a pinch of pecuniary persuasion, for my own slow escape far into the North.

I was somewhat saddened to leave Cuba, not least through thought of the long journey ahead. Nearly all the way we slid easily through the warm waves of the Gulf Stream, the pump that empties the hot pool of Mexico across the open ocean into Europe's cooler coves. But we weren't long within sight of the American coastline, and again unmarked sky, boundless sea and salty air would be our daily portion, myself and the Canadian crew who, through frequent conversation and regular routine, kept each other sane. On we went, for many days, like countless ships before us – from sail to steam to diesel – and far beneath us, who knows how many broken vessels slept, their unfortunate crews having fallen upon less favourable winds? Surely it can only have been the day-to-day running of the ship, the small but certain tasks, that stopped those poor sailors who travelled for so many, many weeks into the unknown, from lapsing into lunacy all those centuries ago. Perhaps Columbus' crew were, after all, a little mad when they reached land at last and did what they did to the West Indian isles.

Not for us, a watery demise in the ocean's frigid bowels – no monster of the unseen miles would taste us, a novel delicacy, this time. But I couldn't help but think of the numerous creatures we might be affecting. Some two thousand cetaceans every year end up dashed and helpless on the shore, made delirious or distracted by the ceaseless thudding of modern ocean-going craft, and many die the slow, painful death of dehydration or collapse in agony under their own weight. My only consolation was that my presence, doing nothing either to hasten or hinder this ship, made no contribution to the noise, nor the chimneys of smoke, nor any watery legacy we left in our wake.

At last, we saw the welcome cliffs of Canada's lengthy coast, made longer by the immeasurable crenulations of its northern fjords and eastern scattering of tiny islands. Disembarking into freezing rain and cold Newfoundland air, we knew we'd come a long way from Cuba's near-constant thirty degree climate. The sun still spilled a smoky glimmer, just about, into the twilit west, but winter was coming in now to the North: the dark days when she hardly rises, and above the Arctic circle there lurks near-perpetual night. My aim now was to see that dying snowscape as its heyday faded into dusk, to watch it once more melt into the darkness of the

160

solstice before this ice-palace really melted, beyond reconstruction, into a salty pool. The heady heat of humanity's busy world lay behind and beneath me; above me awaited the miserable consequence of its most devastating mistake. A deep gloom fell over my heart as I gathered my pack, stepped onto the slushy soil, and vanished into the dusk.

## 17: Tension
### *The Frozen North*

The North wasn't designed for travellers. Even in a warming world, where my arrival was met with bitterly weeping rain that would have been snow in a more typical November – if 'typical' still exists any more – Canada is not a country easily traversed. As I wended my slow way northwards, the darkness descending like a closing curtain, the muddy land relapsed at last to crystal snow, and I felt more and more an alien, on a harsh planet emptying of life. My direction, needle north by hitch-hike, foot and crook, was dead against the flow: into the desolate lands lately abandoned by summer birds escaping to the south. 'South'. Even the word became a warming balm: the memory of sweet sunshine on green hillsides, golden light amidst the glades. Never in my travels had I missed my temperate homeland more.

Yet on I went, slipping on a thicker coat against the cold that bit my hands red. Steadily the settlements grew sparser, the snowy roads less frequented, but I found my way to a place to sleep, somehow, each night. I had to keep moving. The days were growing shorter; soon it would be too late. Deep in so cold a country, perhaps it wasn't surprising that few of the drivers who lent me a lift seemed worried about climate change. They knew it was happening alright: the signs were all around. More and more years of later than average autumn snow; earlier and earlier springtime melt. But in the bleak midst of an Arctic winter such facts offer little consolation against the freezing air. Indeed, some welcome the warming summers and the melting ice.

Canada is a land of rich resources, but until now its frigid northern seas have been spared the pitiless pounding of mechanised extraction. Maybe not for much longer: the oil giants have sniffed out precious reserves of that foul fluid beneath the Beaufort Sea, and would be eager to cash in on this discovery. Some I came across looked forward to longer spells of open seas, more jobs, more trade, more money pouring in. But for the indigenous peoples of these ice lands, climate change could mean the destruction of an entire way of life. There's a deep tension here, growing like a fissure through a calving ice-shelf – the need to protect a precious place and the precious life that inhabits it, tugging against the desire to grow, to prosper, to embrace the change.

But there's one spectacle that will never alter. Day by day, the sun began to flounder in its vain attempts to clamber up the sky, and when a couple in a snow-capped four-by-four offered me a spare seat, I joined their journey on the new track up to the northern coast. There, amidst the calm surroundings of a huddled Inuit settlement, I saw the sea at last again before me, glistening in the pale light so soon after dawn. Looking back towards the south, the orange glimmer of the sun flashed and retreated, as though, frightened or disgusted at the world it glimpsed, it didn't think it worth the effort to take a proper look. It was the last day of

November. Before we left I gazed through the twilight at the northern horizon, making out the faint form of Baffin Island, Canada's largest, and reportedly one of the most beautiful gems in the country's crumbled constellation of landmasses. There, I knew, the sun wouldn't rise again until January. I wished dearly to travel to that island, to see its famed bestiary of Arctic Wolves and Foxes. But I could not venture any further, into the Polar Night of the Arctic Circle. No boats traverse that treacherous sea at this time of year. The island is isolated – except of course by plane.

It seems to me a saddening irony that the communities of both northern Canada and the 'ground zero' of climate change itself, Greenland, are so dangerously dependent on one of the most-wanted criminals on the global warming hit-list, the aeroplane. Those mitigation target-busting beasts scratch their scores of scars across the Arctic sky, seemingly impervious to the dwindling glaciers and drowning lands beneath them, in whose demise they play a princely part, smashing the very vessels of masterfully crafted ice the visitors they carry have often come to see. Canada has the longest coastline in the world, but its rate of coastal erosion is equally impressive. The Beaufort Sea swallows a metre of land a year, but where the stormy winds stir up still more energetic waves, up to twenty metres can vanish in just a few months. The culprit isn't hard to see: wilder weather and melting permafrost conspire to concoct a saline soup of destruction that threatens homes, supplies of food and fresh water and survival itself for the human and other animal inhabitants of this surprised ecosystem. The Inuit have used sea ice for transport for thousands of years; now these waters will instead be the domain of dirty diesel cruisers, as the Arctic is unlocked – tamed of its cold, inhospitable sharpness; stripped of its snowy beauty. It's already warming at twice the average global rate.

Slow travel north being impossible, I took the next best course and headed west: with a little light persuasion, the owner of a wind-battered fishing boat was willing to take me across the Hudson Bay. We set out as soon twilight crept across the sky, shivering as we swept over the cold, grey waters that looked even less forgiving than the land. Delayed by the relatively mild start to the season, this was perhaps the last boat back across this splinter of sea. The stars made their never-ending circle overhead, a polar breeze rattled on the sail, and as the celestial backdrop so soon blackened again into night, I caught my first sight of the Northern Lights swimming like a mirage in the sky. The magic of those few minutes was worth every second of the long, slow struggle I'd had to get there.

It was well after dark when we arrived in Churchill, a town on the frontier of the great winter freeze. I was told to keep my eyes peeled for its most infamous inhabitants, and wasn't disappointed. Some brash young polar bears had snuck in to raid this, their sweetest honey-pot, where their kind are forced increasingly to scavenge on the streets when ice and

165

access to food is scarce. These tired, hungry creatures were late for their hibernation, still on the prowl for a few final morsels to feed their cubs. Amazing animals, the Kings of the Arctic grew fat on the fruit of its heyday; now they are reduced to beggars stealing crumbs from a species that proved to be the more powerful beast. The relationship between bear and man, struggling to live alongside each other, is under increasing strain. But I saw no more of them; in a couple of days it was time to board on one of Canada's few railroads, to be whisked to Winnipeg and along Canada's southern belt of cities, then north again to find the country's chilly western fringe.

## 18: Myth
*From Canada to Russia*

A vast and varied wonderland of unimagined splendour. Such new, dramatic sights of spectacle had few parallels on the pages of sweet, well-tempered Europe or age-old sun-scorched North Africa's well-thumbed manuscripts. It's no wonder the dumbfounded explorers, stumbling upon this immense set of scenes unseen, this blank book far, far across the Western sea, called it a 'New World'. Only trundling by train, east to west for many days right across North America's extensive girth, can the fantastic magnitude of this impressive continent be somewhat understood. Such great excitement this discovery must have instilled: a fancied dream become reality, a lost land leaping out of legend onto the empty edges of the map.

On my own cross-Canadian journey in midwinter, I fancied the scenery was no less splendid than in summer's leafy-green garb. For me, the sturdy evergreens were dusted with snow; ice-white mountains encircled murky pools of mystery, wide lakes brimming with the silver blood of glaciers made molten by many summers' heats. To experience the full gravity of these magnificent places, I travelled slowly, breaking up my long train journey to walk deep into mountain vales and hear the snow-white silence and breathe the cool clean air. But gradually I wended west and north, in the footsteps of those first explorers of my ilk who discovered these lands but a few hundred years before me, but in the opposite direction to their distant predecessors, the first human feet to tread these stones countless generations before. I was headed for the Bering Strait, the narrow tempestuous torrent that forms the hair-fine fissure between two colossal continents, which in a younger, colder Earth were linked by an arc of ice.

But first, to cross Alaska. My Canadian train brought me not to the Alaskan land border, but to Port Arthur, where though the snow and ice were gathering and the trees and birds less numerous than further south, the inhospitable Arctic did not quite have dominion and the sea wasn't frozen shut. There, it was possible to transfer to a train ferry – an old-fashioned means of transportation quite new to me – and, rolling by rail straight onto a boat, we made a short and sunny crossing to American shores, before rolling off again to continue on our way. Similarly seductive scenery awaited me, and, carried by train at last I briefly crossed the Arctic Circle, coming – not long before the winter solstice – to the very edge of the land of perpetual winter dark.

Another beautiful aurora burst to life before me that first nearly never-ending night, a mesmerising spectacle brought on by sparkling streams of stardust, but said in Norse mythology to be the sheen of armour worn by Odin's Valkyrie army as it marched across the sky. I witnessed too the strange sight of high, eerie glowing polar clouds in the dim twilight, with the sun's light gently growing almost to the dawn. The hidden fire hung tantalisingly just beyond the horizon, but withdrew again, his promise unfulfilled. I paused there, in that starlit land, while the deepest dark of winter idled by, alleviated, even there, by the joyful festivities of that special time of year. Then, as the final embers of 2018 began to fade away, I boarded another train to continue on my way.

This journey would have been impossible even a year before. But in contrast to the tightening noose being tugged on all America's other borders, here I was gifted by a sole migration loosening effected by its ersatz president: the bridging, at last, of the cold chasm betwixt the United States and her near Asian neighbour, Russia. Though it is possible to cross the Bering Sea by foot, if one is willing to take one's chances over the shifting ice-floats that wobble like sliding stepping-stones all through its stormy, wind-swept breadth, this border has been closed to travellers from afar for decades. A manned military Russian base oversees Big Diomede Island in its midst, and the few who have made it, in recent years, to the far side have been met by arrest and expulsion. But my journey came soon after the completion of a project dreamt of over a century before, and brought to fruition at last by the mutual friends that lead these once-warring states: a great train line linking, by bridge and tunnel, Russia and America. So it is that I can return the way those ancient humans came, albeit by somewhat swifter means. Looking out from the safety of a railway carriage, I beheld beneath swelling waters of one of the most dangerous straits in the world, and passed safely across.

How long this cordiality will last is anybody's guess in such uncertain times. Arriving in the Russian province of Chukotka, it was as though I peered beneath a veil into a secret, forgotten corner that had been, until so recently, still in the shadow of the Cold War. There were no roads here, no shops, no restaurants, in a society not spoiled by streams of tourists. Apart from brief arrivals on the new cross-continental train, this is Russia's 'last closed territory', with no free travel and the strict entry requirements that each visitor obtains a special visa and a sponsor from amongst the inhabitants – who must promise to keep watch on them night and day.

This bitter landscape, with temperatures at this time of year swaying between 15 and 35 degrees below zero – was inhabited by an ancient Chukchi people long before the Russians arrived in 1641. They remain a society steeped in Shamanist ritual and myth, telling strange stories of ancient battles and Earth's creation, seeing spirits in animals, forests, rivers and stars. To me and my fellow travellers – set down but for a few hours by the train – they showed generosity and welcome, offering us food and shelter in their traditional yarangas or more modern wood or concrete soviet-era single-storey blocks. Most of the people are reindeer herders, fishermen or whalers, carrying on long-lived ways of life that Russian influence could not quite dispel, refreshingly at odds with the rest of the world that seems in some respects more like to a separate universe.

But there are signs, inevitably, of a grimmer reality stamped upon the province, carried here by the greedy machinations of the USSR. Here and there the landscape is pocked by the blight of industrial complexes, designed to extract and process the gas, coal, gold and tungsten treasures that hide beneath these hills and perhaps in some way compensate for the great reserves of oil Russia lost unknowingly to America when she sold Alaska. Somewhere, also, in that bleak expanse, disused rails run to hidden horrors, the gulags of the Stalinist Terror where political prisoners from across this huge country were forced to face the winter freeze in slavery and suffering for their supposed sins. Despite the warmth of the locals, something more than the chill Arctic breeze was making me shiver inside, and it was not with regret that, the short sojourn over, I was asked to re-embark the train and continue on my way.

## 19: Bodies
*Across Russia*

Like a great, central artery the Trans-Siberian Railway sweeps right across the vast expanse of Russia the giant. From Vladivostok in the East to Moscow in the West, through snowy plains and forested mountains, crossing countless streams with names unknown to travellers overwhelmed by so great a swiftly sweeping, vanishing array, it can convey you in less than a week from end to end. Joining this aged network from its newest, northern limb on my slow cross-country journey across the 'Second World', I stopped some third of the way westwards in the sub-polar city of Irkutsk. That city, in itself, proved a place of little splendour, save for its exquisite gaily-coloured Orthodox churches still stamping a magical and distinctly Russian character upon a settlement rendered somewhat drab by Soviet-era changes. Here are ugly twentieth-century buildings – assaults against the art of architecture just as atrocious as any other turgid post-war tower-blocks in the West or in the East.

But what I'd really come for was every bit the gleaming gem of Russian natural beauty that I'd been promised it would be. Surrounded by mountains that predate the dinosaurs, atop a seven-kilometre-deep sediment-filled rift that stood the test of thirty million years, lies the largest, deepest, oldest body of fresh water on Earth: Lake Baikal, 'Nature Lake'. Its waters, also some of the world's clearest, stretch down to a depth of over one-and-a-half kilometres, teeming with life. Gazing in awe upon this glassy expanse, it was difficult to imagine such profound deeps, and the many unique and wonderful works of nature concealed therein. Arriving on an antique, picturesque railway that man made, in a quainter era, to skirt this great mirror of enchanted adoration, I saw its timeless beauty from many angles – except of course from beneath the icy waves.

That I did not submerge my own body within those frigid waters was perhaps just as well: I discovered that the lake may be clear, but it isn't always clean; every year several thousand tonnes of liquid waste disgorge into the crystal waters from bulging boats and tourist resorts that dot the shoreline. For nearly five decades a paper mill pumped in pollutants, threatening the age-old kaleidoscope of life for the sake of empty pages belched out in their blank, faceless reams. And Baikal's very vastness almost made it vulnerable, not long ago, to the threat of an oilier ooze, as profit-pained prospectors sought the quickest path to lay a Russia-China pipeline, right through its sacred waters, carrying with it all the risk of potential leaks and spills. Fortunately, the government stepped in and diverted the pipe just days before its construction, and instead of a paper mill I was greeted by the Baikal Nature Reserve exhibit that's somewhat ironically replaced it. Maybe this special place will survive the murky footprint of recent modernity after all.

Yet if the future's clean and green, Russia certainly hasn't kept up with the times. The contribution of renewable energy to its electricity has been almost static for years, being mostly in the form of decades-old hydroelectric dams. It's commitments under the Paris Climate Change Agreement somewhat craftily constitute a thirty per cent emissions cut by 2030 on the 1990 levels of the filthy USSR, which is actually a rise relative to today. For Russia, fossil fuel is king, and she draws in huge sums selling billions of barrels of oil and voluminous quantities of gas west into Europe and now south, via a new body of pipelines, to a China hungry for energy and eager to abandon even dirtier coal. There are reserves without reckoning lurking beneath Siberia, enough to cause climatic devastation is the world doesn't change its habits and avert an impending apocalypse of its own invention. Russia's whole 'business model' is based on the hope that it will not.

Nor is nuclear power such a promising prospect as it once was set to be. The Trans-Siberian took me on through the rugged Urals region, where Earth's most aged mountains stretch to the sky in a barrier 2500 kilometres long from north to south. The region became, from the twentieth century, Russia's poisoned industrial heart, as factories and people poured east to escape the spectre of German occupation in the Second World War. The mountains are as safe a refuge as any, driving such a cleft that the climate on their Siberia-facing eastern slopes is noticeably different to that of their warmer western fringes. This was where, in the heady rush of wars both hot and cold, Russia sought to develop herself into the world's nuclear superpower. The hideous remnants of a too-hasty dabbling in dangerous physics are still there, supposedly secret but impossible to hide.

The Urals are a place of dark forest and deep mines, beautiful on the surface but hiding ugly truths. My train didn't run through the little town of Kyshtym, site of the world's third worst nuclear disaster in September 1957. For a decade the research centre there had dumped unfiltered radioactive waste into the now hopelessly corrupted Techa River, a tirade of toxic sludge accumulating in a squalid soup in Karachay Lake. When a waste tank was finally installed instead, little care was taken to keep it properly cool. The resulting explosion sent deadly soot settling for miles around. But few knew of the true extent of this hushed-up horror, and some nearby neighbourhoods – though dangerously radioactive – weren't evacuated for over a year. It was not until 1976 that the USSR at last admitted to the rest of the world just why the security of the Kryshtym 'nature reserve' was so strictly enforced. The Techa River still retains thirty times the safe concentration of tritium.

But it wasn't radiation poisoning that filled me with fear for the future as I descended from the Urals, which in many parts remain a wonderland of wildlife despite the industrial incursions. It's worth remembering that many, many more people will die from the toxic fumes spat out by power-stations greedily guzzling Russia's unspent reserves of coal than have died in all the world's nuclear power disasters to date.

175

Air pollution remains the world's biggest premature killer. And that's without even counting the cost of the climate change catalysed by those carbon belching furnaces. If Russia wants lasting prosperity, and to preserve all this beauty for future generations, it's its barmy business model that's going to have to change.

## 20: Fracture
### *In Saint Petersburg*

Saint Petersburg was famously said to be the most 'intentional' city in the world. In some respects it has always resembled more symbol that settlement: the symbol of what its founder, Peter the Great, wanted his Russia to be in 1703; the symbol of an artificially Europeanised 'western' Russian culture under the subsequent Tsars; and yet, through its distinctive World Heritage accredited architecture, surely today the symbol of an archetypically Russian style. Like the unique set of symbols that forms the Russian alphabet, somewhat familiar and yet strikingly different and sometimes surprising to those accustomed to either Latin or Greek scripts, this city-symbol too encompasses echoes of Greek and whisperings of western motifs, yet remains unmistakably and unashamedly Russian.

Even its name has been the political plaything of powers from across the spectrum, eager to use this centrepiece as a tug to veer the vast country to their transient causes. Peter himself consciously aped flashy, modern eighteenth-century Germany with his use of 'burg'; to a twentieth-century Tsardom at war with their western near-neighbour 'Petrograd' proved a more palatable title for the then fiercely self-asserting capital. The biggest name in Soviet Russia was deemed more worthy than Christ's apostle to honour its biggest city, so under Communist jurisdiction 'Leningrad' became for a time the name of the place where Lenin's Winter

177

Palace coup had put paid to short-lived democracy in 1917. When the ballot-box returned – and with it normality – to a land worn out by three quarters of a century of war and fear in 1991, the people voted to put it back to 'Petersburg', perhaps trying by this small act at least to pretend the previous seventy-five years of history hadn't happened.

The city I arrived at, over a hundred years on from the 'communist' coup, appeared not to have been spoiled by so long a time of turmoil. That there are eight thousand designated monuments in this few square miles perhaps best attests to its beauty. Arriving by rail at the site of the first Russian railway, built in 1837, I was stunned by a skyline glittering with colourful domes of the east sprinkled amidst grand boulevards of posh apartments that could pass themselves off almost as natives in Paris or Venice or Vienna. This is home to four million people, housed in large part by a preponderance of more modern buildings that skirt the centre. But for once my eyes needed not be sored by silhouettes of 'skyscrapers' so recklessly enamoured by so many of the world's 'slick' cities – even Gazprom, the heaviest giant in Russia's voluminous gas industry, was thwarted in its efforts to erect such an ugly edifice by popular protest. St Petersburg seemed to me to command a respect not enjoyed by other cultural capitals – even Paris has its Montparnasse and London its shards – perhaps partly as a consequence of the long list of internationally respected people it has produced. Mussorgsky and Stravinsky were born into its melody; the births of

Puskin, Golgol and Dostoyevsky are written in its registers, alongside those of Rasputin and Nobel. Perhaps more importantly these days, Prime Minister Medvedev and President Putin himself are both children of Leningrad.

The ghosts of Soviet past still haunted here, I found, but not all were such frightful phantoms as the biased binoculars of Cold War competition might have rendered them from outside at the time when East seemed irreparably fractured from West. Shared communal apartments, given free to families by the USSR, were still commonplace. That state was repressive, terrifying and frankly uninspiring – of anything but fear – to its imprisoned inhabitants. They gained a lot with its fall in terms of freedom, knowledge and power. But undoubtedly Russians lost something too. The USSR had proudly styled itself a world power, and had at least stood out as radically different from the capitalism that enslaved – albeit less violently – peoples in much of the rest of the world. Resources were, at least in principle, there to be shared, and the achievements possible as a community were lauded over individual attainment.

Now, I found a country still yearning for what Russia has always desired, even since the time of Peter the Great – recognition, respect and acceptance on the world stage – but at the same time still recovering from being labelled the 'loser' of the Cold War and still grappling with, it seemed to me, a certain loneliness as a country now that the old Soviet Republics were no

179

longer united or, for the most part, socialist, enforced community had fallen apart and the reality of life under consumerist western capitalism had been shown up for the disappointing banality that it really was. The clothes were more colourful now, the shops stocked much more fully, but the heart of a life based around money could prove just as cold as the concrete and callousness of the previous prison this people had so gleefully escaped.

As I wondered through the wide streets, however, I heard little talk about big-scale politics or even the controversial foreign policy being used in recent years to put pressure on Russia's former satellite states. There was something of much more pressing concern closer to home. Having all but ignored climatic change thus far, and indeed still doing little to prevent it, Russia had nearly faced the prospect of its most alluring poster-piece city being swallowed by the waves of a terrifying tidal surge, almost breaching the five metre height of the St Petersburg dam, a huge project under construction for thirty-five years before its eventual completion in 2011. The city had flooded before, and it was a surge of nearly three metres most recently in 1975 that spurred the dam's creation. But the seas are rising, and in 2018 high surges were becoming more common. Ultimately, the world was beginning to realise, we might not be able to build a barrier strong enough to stem the storm of our own careless conjuring, and the city's days might be numbered with not many digits. That fear at last, it seemed, was becoming all too real amongst the inhabitants of places on the brink such as this.

It was only at these forefronts of fear that a sense of climatic foreboding began to be made palpable: the sense that at some point in the not-too-distant future the world as we know it would, despite its misplaced confidence in the way things were, fall apart – shattered suddenly to pieces like a fractured windowpane. Sometimes, you can't even see the initial hairline crack when something starts to break. But gradually it grows until it creeps beyond its hidden tipping-point and the whole substantial structure disintegrates at once. It happened to the USSR in 1990. Now it was about to swallow St Petersburg, the Pacific Isles, so many other places that I'd seen. The capitalist culture can't support its own heavy weight indefinitely, I mused. One day, soon, it must change – or it will crack.

## 21: Growth
### Through Mongolia

The winter's freeze was beginning to thaw as I made my way south: into the Heart of Asia. This was the land where Russia and China meet: a large, land-locked expanse surrounded by its powerful neighbours, the mythical heart of an infamous ancient Empire that was the largest contiguous power the world has ever seen. I had discovered the hidden ambrosia of Mongolia. At the outset I found it cold and somewhat bleak; the bare, broken mountain slopes lifting their lofty stores of sparkling snow on either side like slumbering giant guardians of a forgotten paradise. But as the rails rolled me down from these Northern heights, the lively breath of spring began to shake the trees and grasslands from their slumber, and there rose in me a strong desire to desert the air-conditioned discomfort of my Trans-Siberian carriage and venture into the vast, enticing wilderness that seemed to rise about me like a rediscovered Eden.

Mongolia is a land of many contrasts. It shivers under freezing winters in the grip of anticyclonic Siberian air, then bakes in sweltering summers brought on by its continental shelter and so many sunny days. As I set out on foot, leaving the plush modernity of the railway station behind me, I stepped into a world that felt somehow out of touch with the past few hundred years. This was still a largely nomadic country, of isolated rural dwellings and wide pastures. Trusting, perhaps recklessly, to fortune, I turned myself vaguely south, and strode into the crisp spring morning, my lungs brought alive by the sweet, clean air.

I confess that I was somewhat trepidatious, a foreign traveller speaking a foreign tongue, that my wandering would be greeted with bemusement – or even hostility – by those whose lands I trespassed upon. It wasn't long, after leaving the town by the first rugged trail I found, before I came upon my first 'ger' settlement: half-a-dozen traditional, moveable tents of wood and white wool-felt huddled lightly upon the hillside. Some cattle were grazing idly nearby, and in the glittering sunshine the sight seemed somewhat idyllic; almost I could forget the modern worries of climatic change, pollution, squalor and destruction that hung like heavy burdens on my heart; almost, this place seemed like an escape from the mess of modernity itself. The old woman who, I suddenly realised, had marked my approach and was watching me still, spoke in words whose precise meaning I could not know but whose sentiment it was easy to fathom from her tone and gesture: words of welcome, not of suspicion. Eagerly she offered me refreshment, the first of many such acts of kindly hospitality I witnessed or was myself blessed by on my slow journey southwards.

Though they may not have received many foreign visitors on foot, this travelling people was certainly accustomed to migration. Most of them retained a nomadic, horse- and cattle-culture lifestyle that had survived for centuries, fading into anachronism as the world changed about them while the long years stretched by. It is a long time since Genghis Khan brought this people greatness in war and this land dominated the Eastern world. Now, peace is their practice. There was a long tradition of Buddhism here, and I perceived an abundance of great love alike for man, bird and beast, as well as for the living hills, fields and flora upon which they depend. These people cared deeply for the animals they exploited: not for them any out-sourcing to factory farms or wasteful over-indulgence at their beasts' expense. They took with gratitude, and consciously acknowledged the need to protect and preserve their precious environment throughout all aspects of life. As I moved on through wood and plain, a combination of gestured directions and their willingness to share Nature's gifts of sustenance and shelter brought me safely through this corner of splendour, seemingly unspoiled by modern industry and the love of money.

But, inevitably, modernity must come calling, and after not many days I returned, reluctantly, to urban habitation. Picking up the slithering trail of the Russia-China railway, I set about learning the reality behind the beautiful veneer. In truth, many of these people were under strain: I could see it in their very faces. For all I had enjoyed it, this landscape was, I was warned, far from unthreatened, Mongolia having borne already an unfairly heavy share of the burden of the global warming that others have produced. Its temperature had already risen, on average, by over two degrees Celsius relative to pre-industrial times, and the country was just emerging from another devastating 'dzud' – an especially hot summer followed by a particularly cold winter – something that used to be rare but was becoming alarmingly frequent. Such conditions kill cattle, frazzle grassland and drive herdsmen out of their rural heartlands. In the worst-hit places, piles of animal carcasses still littered the countryside. The autumn, with its renewing rains, had all but disappeared entirely between these vying extremes.

Already nearly half the country's population had congregated at the capital Ulaanbaatar, my next stop, setting up makeshift suburbs with streets of their moveable habitations carried in from the plains. A dirty cloud of smog surrounded the city as the train pulled in, produced by thousands of families burning rubbish to keep warm.

Although this migration was provoked by natural disaster, it would be a mistake to blame only foreign climatic factors. It seems that Siberian air is not the only chill to have extended its cold fingers from the North. From 1924, Mongolia was one of the Soviet Union's satellite states, and under its cruel influence Buddhism was repressed, its adherents rooted out and sometimes killed and its seven-hundred monasteries nearly all destroyed. Meanwhile, many of the ancient forests were logged, a lack of trees and emphasis on increased production saw soils erode and mining was begun.

1990 saw the end of Russian influence, but in some ways the new democratic government made things worse, with its focus on capital and economic growth. Gone are the communal distributions of fodder to ease the dzuds. Gone are the restrictions on animal numbers that prevented overgrazing and, inadvertently, capped methane emissions whilst keeping up animal welfare standards relative to over-populated farms. I found, to my deep distress, a happy and sustainable way of life dying out, needlessly, amidst a storm of many throes, and a people bitterly mourning its passing. The people missed a countryside where all was freely given by Nature and shared according to need, now trapped in a growing city whose main focus is money. As I reached, at last, a whole year since I had first set out on my slow travel to witness for myself the world's woes, to see a society crumbling before my eyes was, perhaps, my most harrowing sight of all.

End of Section 2

## 22: Shift
*Recalling 2017 – a true story*

I have now, in the course of some twenty-one instalments, related to you most of the adventures that awaited me on setting out, so many years ago now it seems like another Age, in the spring of 2018 on my long journey of Slow Travel. Many miles I ventured by foot or boat or train, but always keeping to the living surface of the Earth I held so dear, so as to see as I passed its many peoples, problems and proposed solutions; to bear witness to the damage then being done by a humanity that didn't seem to know what it was doing to itself.

You have learned now, if you have followed my tale, about the black holes of Indian coal mines; the terrifying towers of Eastern cities; the beautiful landscapes from warm Iran to frozen Canada; the islands made of plastic or holding out as havens of socialist optimism. Everywhere I looked I saw the world shifting under the strain of global industrialisation, to which were rapidly falling victim both human cultures and splendours of nature, now long-since scattered into the dust of forgetting – lost in a great extinction that was then only just at its beginning. But now, I beg to pause in my train of recollections of that great journey, for the passage through Mongolia that I have just related has reminded me of an even earlier adventure, one whose cataloguing here might explain to you an outstanding quandary that may have crossed your mind. Namely, how was it that I could set off on so long a travel, eschewing the aeroplane that was the ordinary long-distance means of transportation in those days, and trust that I could nonetheless cross the world without so much as any mobile means of communication?

The answer is that I had done it before – a shorter trip, though no less enlightening while it lasted – for one hot summer fortnight in 2017. I had been summoned, for reasons I have not space to relate, to the far-Eastern city of Singapore, and given an outbound plane ticket to boot. But knowing the great environmental cost of those ill-advised flying machines, belching plumes of pollution as they do into just the place where it can do the most damage; and reflecting on my own ignorance of the colossal continent of Asia, I decided that I had little choice but to organise my own way back over land. And fortunate indeed did my decision prove, for the fourteen hours ordeal I endured in that prison of the sky on my way eastwards I would, with hindsight, willingly swap for many times the fourteen days I spent travelling back westwards by slower means.

The city-state of Singapore in 2017 would have been to any of that city's inhabitants of but a few decades before utterly unrecognisable. Indeed, there I discovered, somewhat depressingly, a country so addicted to change that without constantly constructing new tower-blocks and tunnels, I feared, its economy would have entirely collapsed. To satisfy its huge appetite for building projects sufficient to keep its people employed, the small island was even in the process of physically enlarging itself by 25%, dredging up land to 'reclaim' from the seas. And many of its people not employed in wasting voluminous resources on this task of ultimately purposeless construction – for with a declining birth rate and strict controls on immigration the islanders' need for living-space was likely to go only down – were kept busy by equally unsustainable industries. Big-money banking, shopping malls that filled labyrinth-like underground streets, an army that held nearly a fifth of the five-million-strong population in reserve, and hedonistic hotels such as a huge ship-like edifice erected by an American billionaire were hardly the sorts of endeavours conducive to any lasting legacy short of copious quantities of squandered resources and greenhouse gas emissions.

Yet somehow my discomfort at all this was alleviated by some small but meaningful measures that showed that Singapore might at least be awakening to the need for change. Nowhere else have I known such careful consideration regarding the use of water – a commodity that was already in short supply – nor such willingness on the part of a people to sacrifice pointless small individual liberties in pursuit of the freedom to live in a healthier society. Chewing gum was banned; cars were taxed so heavily they cost more than houses; those living near their parents were rewarded with lower rents in government-owned housing to thank them for providing social care. And the people were proud to call Singapore the 'city within a garden', with numerous trees planted to partly compensate the huge

Heat Island effect and a large patch of pristine forest still extant.

The tidiness of Singapore, in public attitude as well as visual aspect, was conspicuously absent when I crossed the narrow road-bridge into its much bigger and messier sister, Malaysia. The timing of my journey was, in retrospect, ill, for I had chosen a weekend of holiday in Malaysia, and at the border bus station in Singapore I found myself alone amidst a sea of ethnic Malaysians on their way to visit relatives or shop for cheap goods and chewing gum. Coach after coach for these travellers came rattling past us in that underground space, clogging up the road and our lungs, before the long-awaited public bus at last battled its way through. I was lucky to get to Johor Bahru in time for my train.

But it was worth the effort, for now I came to one of the most pleasant parts of my Singapore to Oxford journey: a long ride on the slow train to Gemas in the hot morning sun. The guard hadn't bothered to close the doors, in spite of signs warning of a thousand Ringgit fine for opening them while the train was in motion, so I stood at the doorway while the fresh Malaysian air – and the occasional earthy smell of dung used as fertiliser – wafted over me. The train jolted and screeched down the rusty single track, through lofty palm plantations and snatches of forest they've largely replaced. Gemas seemed a ghost town, deserted in the afternoon heat; there, alas, I had to swap my aged branch-line loco for the illness-inducing air-conditioned capsule of a modern electric train. Now, televisions in every carriage bore adverts for 'magic flour' of the just-add-water variety and other imported western poisons, while an automated announcement described what to do in an emergency in a creamy American accent above soppy saxophone music more suited to a call-centre that had put you on hold. Meanwhile outside showery rain was falling, and Malaysia passed by seen but no longer smelt – shut off behind the tightly sealed glass. I shivered, and not just because of the absurdly-set air conditioning. On simply crossing between platforms I'd felt first-hand one of the many sad shifts being parcelled out as 'progress' here. To me, it felt more like suffocation.

## 23: Gravity
*Thailand – a true story*

'Hotel,' said the border official, pointing to the place I'd left blank on the form. I must have looked conspicuously European as I waited amidst the queues of Malaysians to cross into Thailand, for almost at once he had come and beckoned me into a side office. Britons, as I knew, did not need a Thai visa, but I wasn't going to get across without filling in the proper paperwork.

'No hotel,' I said, trying to explain that I'd be sleeping on the train, just passing through Thailand on my way north.

'Ah. You sleep on the train. Where you go? Bangkok? You must put your hotel in Bangkok.'

'But I'm not staying in Bangkok. I catch another train – to Laos.'

After a little persistence in this vein, he seemed to understand. 'Ah, I see. Not stay in Thailand. You sleep on the train.' He paused. 'But you must put down hotel. No hotel…' – he held out his hands emphatically– 'no come in to Thailand. You go back to Malaysia.'

The man sat back, waiting expectantly. 'Put down hotel.'

Now, at last I understood what he wanted me to do. I wrote slowly on the paper, thinking desperately of a place to invent, 'Hotel Bangkok'. He took the paper, and looked at it. Then he handed it back. 'There is no Hotel Bangkok.'

Again, he waited. I was now feeling very nervous, as the gravity of the situation grew upon me. Would this be the end of my journey, already? How would I get back? Carefully, and in full sight of the man, I crossed out what I had written and wrote instead, 'Hotel International Bangkok'. He took the paper, read it, and stamped my passport. It had done the trick, it seemed. I was let in.

I was on my way into Thailand from Malaysia, in whose capital Kuala Lumpur I'd stopped off for the night. Emerging from Kuala Lumpur's enclosed modern railway station, you could be forgiven for not knowing which country you were in, let alone how to navigate across a minefield of shops to find the exit, or where to go when you finally found fresh air. The day had been overcast and the sun shrouded, so that when I found my way out I was left with little means of navigation. Confronted with nothing but the cavernous mouth of the carpark under a huge hotel, and a taxi rank attached to a road too narrow to safely walk down, which lead only onto the mass of ring-roads that tangle this city like a deadly knot of snakes, I was trapped. To chance these roads by foot being seemingly too treacherous, I was compelled to take a taxi, which here entailed buying a ticket in advance from a nearby counter. When I did, eventually, find a place to be set down and explore, I found very little worth the risk of the roads. The city appeared to have been transformed in recent years, spotted with skyscrapers that had sprung up like a pox, and cloaked in repugnant air made poisonous by endless streams of diesel cars and busses.

Traffic lights could not be trusted when crossing roads; only in 'China Town' was there an absence of cars, where instead an almost impassable throng of stalls selling plastic tat and packed with people barred the way. The few remnants of cultural heritage were hidden away behind already-crumbling modern constructions, like the 'historic', original railway station whose long, wide platforms now stood largely empty beneath its majestic colonial architecture, relegated to a little-used stop-off for trains going north. It was fashionable, in 2018, for every capital city to possess a metro, and it seems that Malaysia didn't want to be left behind, whether its people wanted one or not. On very ugly concrete tracks hoisted above the fumes of the city, a shiny modern monorail ran a little-used service, which bore me back to the modern station in a tiny – and almost empty – capsule train. It seemed quite evident that Kuala Lumpans preferred the car.

English was widely spoken in Malaysia, and a Briton might enjoy the familiar comforts of English-style sockets and cars driving on the left. But my journey was about to became more adventurous when my train drew me up to the last stop in Malaysia – the oversized terminus at Padang Besar – and I walked across the border into Thailand. Few Thai speak English, and I certainly didn't know any Thai, so broken phrases and gestures were to be the only means of communication. Just as well, then, that the locals were so friendly, not least the border policeman whose helpful hints had let me in.

Padang Besar was a beautiful, rustic town that – save for some small supermarkets – seemed largely to have been unchanged by recent years, with a makeshift market congregating on the dusty unpaved road. A man on a motorbike just past the border insisted he would take me to the town centre, which contained the Thai railway station a couple of miles away from the Malaysian one where I'd arrived. With some trepidation I agreed to climb up behind him, my heavy pack still on my back, and in this precarious balance we went zooming to the town. On our arrival, I fumbled amidst my collection of currencies searching for 50 Thai Baht with which to pay him. Suddenly he seemed to recognise a 500 note, took it and zoomed off, I thought, in search of some change. For a few minutes, standing there alone, I wondered whether I'd accidentally given away a rather hefty tip, but sure enough he soon returned – only to say that the note was no good. Meanwhile I'd found a smaller denomination, with which he seemed satisfied. So, with a few hours to spare, I explored the settlement in the hot afternoon sun, but oddly nobody would accept the large-denomination note, and I was directed to several currency exchanges, all in vain, before taking a proper look at the note – and realising that it wasn't Thai Baht at all, but 500 Russian roubles.

The Thai railway station was efficiently and pleasingly built, consisting of a single platform for the single line, neatly and beautifully decorated, with a staffed station building attached. There was also, as at all Thai stations, a huge portrait of one of the royal princes commanding adoration in a well-kept shrine. I went up to counter, as previously instructed, to collect my ticket, only to be told that my instructions had been wrong: the ticket was supposed to be collected at the Malaysian station, back over the border. Just as I was considering with horror the prospect of returning through the border-checks and having to explain a return to Malaysia and re-entry into Thailand to the border policeman, the station manager thankfully reached for the telephone, and arranged for the ticket to be brought over by motorbike. So it was that, these setbacks avoided with more than a little help from the locals, I boarded the little weather-beaten sleeper train – a gift 'from the people of South Korea', said a plaque, from 1996 – and set off into the sunset.

## 24: Memory
*Vietnam – a true story*

Through the green heart of Thailand we had rushed, where the hills erupt like forested thimbles or rounded dice scattered across the plain: a mesmerising memory of a land where Earth still stores some beleaguered secrets amidst her lofty nooks. The train snipped the undergrowth, charging over little-serviced rails. Yet, sluggish seemed our final approach into the city of contrasts, famed Bangkok, where she lazily listed through thickets of slum shacks. People lived, and slept, and ate, right against the rails; children and dogs stole freely across the tracks, while a filthy stream of sewage sweated in the sun.

But more hideous even than this was the contrast with the concrete metropolis through which my feet soon were wearily to walk, journeying into richer quarters. There, I met with a concrete veneer designed to hide the squalor swept either side of the swanky squares and doorways of the city's rotten heart. A rich-man's metro ran there, spacious and underused. It didn't call at the slums. The city stank of car dust and the impoverishment of 'growth'. Fast food counters thronged with members of the new middle class, crowded into artificial environments as cold as the steel that bore their ugly foreign signs. But I eschewed these evil eateries, following my inner compass away from the cars and the queues and the crude plastic tat piled up in

197

consumerist shrines, back to the jungle of alleyways on the older side of town.

There, I found an open home with empty tables set for food, and a proud proprietor waiting with a welcome and a smile: the lone woman was host and cook, who warmed a healthy mix of fresh green leaves and spices in her huge wok. Served with simple staples of water and rice that cooled a thirsty tongue, it tasted all the sweeter for the added hospitality stirred liberally into the mix, a flavour that I feared would soon be all too hard to find in a world at risk of destroying the things we really held most dear.

Another night train carried me on, to arrive early in the morning where Thailand expires into its northern neighbours close to Laos' capital, Vientiane. A river runs between the two countries, spanned by a railway bridge that we were borne across by a small shuttle train, a little bunch of tourists and travellers from far-flung places congregating at this crossing-point that the locals little used. They filled her up with a hosepipe and the little train sputtered into life, so that soon we were transported to the tiny terminus of Laos' only railway link: the end of the line. All that awaited there was a small customs office, placed with the sole purpose of collecting thirty-five US dollars from each passing traveller as payment for entering Laos.

Vientiane was a city unlike any other. Although undeniably Asian, and packed with amazing temples that gleamed in white and gold on almost every street, it had some of the aroma of the quainter parts of Paris.

French displaced English as the barely-spoken second language; cafes displaced the street-stalls predominant elsewhere and French bread was for sale instead of rice. As an obvious foreigner, everywhere I went I was thronged with calls of 'Put-put! Put-put!' and none of the numerous drivers of these expensive machines seemed satisfied that I'd rather walk than catch a lift. The centrepiece of this ex-colonial town, still extant but surrounded now by much newer creations, was a relic of far former days: a curious man-made mountain that must have towered over the low buildings of its time, but now, tucked away in its quiet corner, forgotten by the passing traffic.

The city had become a place of comings and goings, where every third shop was a currency exchange. It was there that I met the Talkative American, a left-wing pro-peace and anti-Trump traveller, living in self-imposed exile in South-East Asia where he hoped to hide from what his country was becoming. He reminisced about the Vietnam war, the crisis in American democracy and the sad reality of America's xenophobic wing, sipping his cold beer in a veranda-café. 'You'll like Hanoi,' he said when I'd told him my next stop. In this he would be wrong.

The only route from Laos to Vietnam is by road, and it was on a twenty-four-hour bus journey that I found myself that night. Once the young men manning the bus had at last contented themselves that there would be no more passengers and allowed us to set off, through the dark hours of the night we crawled our way upwards past buildings with three walls (it's too warm to need a fourth) at one of which we stopped. There, at once people appeared and set food for their travelling customers on servery-tables, while Vietnamese pop blared out from a television set.

It seemed we were in a race with the other bus companies, to see who'd be first at the border crossing. We must have arrived in the early hours of the night, for when I woke at sunrise we were parked up and second in the queue at the rainy mountain pass, waiting for the border to re-open for the day at seven o' clock. It seemed like hours by the time we'd handed in our passports in a chaotic rabble and been let through the Laos border, re-boarded the bus and gone through the whole process again at the Vietnamese end, where we each had to pay 1 US dollar for the cost of the compulsory passport stamp. No other currency would do.

The place was indeed beautiful, and the windy road ran down through high forests and rural villages where peasants worked in picturesque fields and red hammer-and-sickle banners adorned every street. For all the human and environmental cost of the Vietnam War, the Americans never did stamp out the communism that was still entrenched here with self-conscious zeal. When the mountain scenery was swapped for towns and ugly highways, the all-day journey became somewhat more tedious, but my destination proved to be no more pleasant. Disembarking at last, I set off with eager steps to find Hanoi's railway station, but had I paid proper attention to the scale on the map might have been less optimistic.

Mile after mile I plodded through air thicker with fumes than any I'd known, whether beside the crowded main road or in the quainter side-streets, largely as a result of the huge swarms of autobikes that roared around every corner. I wouldn't heed these drivers either, as they advertised 'Auto! Auto!', refusing to myself become a party to this poisonous air. But when after some time I checked for directions from a helpful young woman keen to practise her English, I found the station to be still many, many miles away. She helped me to find the correct bus to take me, and even insisted on paying the (small) fare. It was in gestures like this that my hope for that, my own floundering generation, was founded. Therein survived a far older kindness, one that gives without the possibility or expectation of reward: a spark of human sympathy, amidst all the noise and smoke.

## 25: Resolution
*China to Russia – a true story*

The representative of the Vietnamese travel company was most apologetic. 'We could not get your ticket to Beijing,' she said. 'Only to Nanning. You can buy the Beijing ticket in Nanning. We will refund your Beijing ticket.' So that was that. It was nine o' clock at night; the Nanning train would leave in half an hour. All of a sudden, whether I'd get to Beijing in time, and thence get home, was thrown into doubt. There was little choice but to take the train and trust it would work out.

For such a huge city, Hanoi's railway station was tiny – perched on an outskirt corner, with a single platform and a waiting room barely big enough to hold a hundred people, it hardly seemed the epitome of an international terminus. Crossing the Chinese border wasn't exactly fun; woken to disembark in the middle of the night, we stood in long queues to go through both checkpoints, where many of the border officials also seemed lately roused from sleep. I could tell already that China was going to be somewhat different: at no other border crossing have I been asked to select from a scale of cartoon faces, from wide smile to heavy frown, to rate my experience and the friendliness of the staff. I must admit, I was impressed.

Indeed, my first taste of China, those unexpected few Thursday hours in Nanning, did not disappoint. I wasn't supposed to have stopped off for long there at all, but perhaps unsurprisingly the high-speed onward

202

connection to Beijing was sold out; fortunately, there were still spaces on another, slower service at five o' clock that night that would still have me in the capital, thousands of miles away, within twenty-four hours. Given that I had to pick up the ticket for the next leg of my journey before Beijing's offices closed for the weekend the next day at 6, this was cutting it fine – but I had no other option.

Nanning was busy and bustling, and very difficult to navigate amidst a peppering of high-rise offices and malls, but by now I was used to that. What really impressed me was the way in which China, somehow, seemed to have retained an authenticity amidst the western-style high-rises that other countries' megacities had lost. Then, there was the relatively clean air. Gone were the puffs of petrol smoke ruining many other Asian cities; all here was electric, silent and clean. This certainly gave me cause for hope in China's age of ascendency, when it was soon to become the foremost superpower charting the course of the world. Furthermore, there was the friendliness of everyone I met, from the special foreign-languages attendant at the station who booked for me my new train to the man who, in spite of my hopeless Chinese pronunciation, helped me to find the Internet Café.

Keeping touch, even occasionally, with home was a perennial problem in that age when everyone else seemed to possess a 'mobile telephone' capable of facilitating world-wide communications, for there was no longer much call for public telephones or computers.

The Internet Café I eventually tracked down was full of Chinese teenagers playing an internet fast-action game, and the helpful proprietors logged me onto a foreign Virtual Private Network to get past the Chinese firewall blocking 'Google Mail'.

Many of the same benefits I found also in Beijing. The journey brought me from the beautiful misty southern hills, where green pastures were turned to gold by the setting Asian sun, into China's eastern industrial heartland. It was made all the more pleasant by two out of the country's billion-plus inhabitants with whom I happened to share a compartment, who despite the language barrier almost seemed to become like friends. But when we arrived, all were dispersed: our faces melting away again into the innumerable crowd.

It was raining, extremely heavily. The long queues to pass security checks on the underground held me up, and when I eventually found the office holding my ticket, it was closed. I tried in vain to find my hotel. Drenched through and alone in the darkness, official infrastructure having failed me, again it was only chance human kindness that got me through. Another young woman practising her English saw that I was lost, and showed me my hotel. The woman at reception let me use the telephone, and what's more my contact at the ticket office answered out of hours and let me rearrange the collection. Three small kindnesses, that made all the difference.

When the next day dawned bright and clear, the beautiful historic buildings of Beijing sprang into life, not crowded nor diminished by their more modern surroundings, and the world seemed somehow much more hopeful. China is a country that cares about heritage, as witnessed by the huge crowds of tourists queuing up at the Forbidden City and thronging Tiananmen Square. Indeed, the only place I found to be utterly deserted was Mao's mausoleum – an indication, perhaps, of the People's true feelings for their Republic's founder.

It was a fond farewell that I bade that evening to the ancient splendour at the heart of the world's upcoming capital. A small group of passengers congregated at the permitted waiting point in Beijing station – woe betide one who tries to descend to a Chinese platform before the train is called – for the 23:00 Moscow departure, boarding the characteristic red-and-silver Russian tin-can carriages of the Trans-Siberian Express. So began a six-day journey across as many time-zones, through the baking heat of the south Siberian summer, at the end of which we arrived only two minutes late. The line had not quite the romance with which it's sometimes been portrayed. The grumpy stewardesses that shouted angrily if one hadn't returned to the train within five minutes of departure at the scheduled stops; the rustic Russian stations where one could wander unimpeded across the tracks and vendors greeted the train with supermarket trolleys full of produce for sale; the deserted restaurant car that offered little else than boiled potatoes and mushrooms, until they also ran out of those; all these added to the charm.

Pulling out of a run-down, dusty town just over the Russian border that was perhaps the poorest I'd seen on all my Asian travels, they played the National Anthem through the station loudspeakers while a few migrating Russian families were waved off into the west. We'd waited for four hours while the train's wheels were changed from Chinese to Russian gauge and the fierce Russian border police had boarded the train with dogs. The length of my hair wasn't consistent with my passport photograph it seemed, and the officer took all of ten minutes to decide it was really me – not a problem, oddly, at the previous thirteen border checkpoints. One sensed something of a nervousness about the Russian border in this sparse-populated region worried about potential overspill from its rapidly growing neighbour in the south.

The heavy rain had followed me to Moscow, as I made my trek across a capital that seemed, by comparison, poorer and shabbier than its Eastern counterparts, helped again by happy chance to find my place of rest. From Red Square, it was onwards to Belarus, Berlin, Brussels, and home: two weeks by train from Singapore, almost entirely on time. I knew I was back in Britain when an 'earlier signal fault' held up my train at Paddington for an hour, which gave me time to muse. It had been a journey to remember, and I resolved to return.

## 26: Wave
*Return to China*

How curious it is, my friends, that my memories should remain so vivid of the far distant journeys that I made so many decades ago. I have now recalled to you that first happy adventure I had, in the long-ago summer of 2017, which so piqued my yearning for exploration and magnified my fears about the short-sighted ways in which the world was then engaged. Before that brief digression, I was explaining to you the course of my longer Slow Travel excursion that that first trip incited: when, in the spring of 2018 I set out, by slow but steady means, to discover the reality at the root of rumours then circulating about a changing world and catastrophe to come. How naïve we were, in those heady, Halcyon days! How proud the strut before this bitter fall! Perhaps you find my tale incredible, so difficult is it now after the long march of years to comprehend such stupidity, such ravaging and waste! So priceless an ornament, of which you and I can now only dream, we held then in our hands, but scarcely saw its beauty before it was irreparably shattered, crushed by the grip of greedy fingers.

I shall resume my tale where I left it, a year into my long Slow Travel journey, at the beginning of April, 2019, in Ulaanbaatar. For a traveller coming south by rail and foot from Russia, there is only one way onwards through Mongolia: down into the Gobi desert, and back into China, through which I had travelled but a few months before. We pulled into the Chinese border-town of Erenhot in the mid-morning, for the customary stopover while the wheels were changed from Russian to Chinese gauge. I was glad to be there at that time of the year, which presented a happy medium between extremes in a barren desert climate that plunged to twenty degrees Celsius below zero in January and climbed well above thirty on a typical day in July. Now, in spring, the desolate plains and bare mountains were at, I suppose, their least bleak, for a land where little rain ever falls and little vegetation ever tries to brave the dusty, salty soil. I was surprised that some hundred thousand inhabitants managed to survive in this desert settlement, but the population had proliferated fifty-fold in a quarter of the century before, brought in to facilitate trade after the easing of restrictions when the USSR fell.

More interesting to me than this dusty town was the story of what some of the Chinese were attempting nearby, at the fringes of the desert. The Great Green Wall, a project that already had a forty year history when I visited in 2019, was a vain and desperate government-sponsored attempt to hold back the encroaching wilderness from the pasture-land beyond, over a thousand square miles of which were already being lost every year. The reason for this desertification was clear: decades of logging to convert sparse forest to flat grassland had opened the Gobi borders to bitter winds that stirred up dust storms, destroying the remaining vegetation. Now, the Chinese aimed to increase forest cover from five to fifteen per cent, hoping that a new Great Wall of trees would break the storms, secure the soil and hold back an invasion just as frightening as that of the barbarian hordes their ancestors were desperate to repel.

What I saw was not encouraging. Acre after acre of monoculture trees that offered little to local wildlife; the two-thousand, eight-hundred mile stretch still far from finished; and ugly grey, empty trunks – like spectres of the winter still haunting the spring – that occupied vast patches where the hastily-planted trees had simply died. These trees were not designed for this desert, nor were its few native animal inhabitants likely to benefit from this alien sort of forest. I would not have been surprised, had I been told then that the venture would prove ultimately unsuccessful, and indeed the Gobi did keep growing, whatever man might do. We were hubristic in those days. We thought we could control the world, or at least predict how our actions would change it. Only subsequent events have proven just how wrong we were.

It was time to move on from Asia. I was told that there was another Great Green Wall taking shape with more success in the Sahara, and my mind soon turned to that first human continent, the northern stretches of which that largest of deserts dominates. But I had now seen all that I could stomach, for now, of the Northern Hemisphere, where up until then I had spent my entire life. There were boats from Beijing, I found, that would take me to the more southerly stretches of the still mysterious giant triangle in the middle of the map: it was time to sail south at last, into Africa.

Another lengthy voyage awaited me, as I boarded the huge European cargo ship making its months-long journey home via southern Africa, even though I was to be disembarking at the first port of call after Asia. The sea-sickness that would previously plague me after even a few hours on a mirror-smooth sea had fortunately already been cured by the weeks spent boating to Hawaii from Japan, yet still the prospect didn't please me, as a lover of land and of roaming far on foot. I had one of only half a dozen passenger cabins – this sort of slow travel was not a popular undertaking – and ate my meals with the crew but otherwise was left alone to read, to write, to ponder and to miss the sight of land.

Nevertheless, the journey was surprisingly pleasant. I found again, on that unending trip, a tranquillity that cannot be obtained except on long sea voyages. For days on end, there was nothing but the endless, rolling waves of the warm Indian Ocean, stretching interminably in all directions as the sun sailed slowly between two empty horizons, from utter east to farthest west. I had no means of communication even to tempt me to contact the wider world, which might as well have ceased entirely to exist. This was what it was, I reasoned, to pioneer the unmapped seas of old, cresting the blue-green wilderness as flotsam on the waves, not knowing what – if anything – awaited on the farther shore of this gigantic lake. The world now seemed wide again – wide and wild, beyond the bounds of human habitation. Home and ground were alien, like an ambrosial dream or fantasy that ceased to be reality in a world composed of water, its only inhabitants the seldom-passing other ships and strange sea creatures dancing on the surf. This experience was at once imprisonment and escape, inspiration and despair. For those who manned humanity's thousands of long-haul freighters, it was a day-to-day normality all seasons of the year. For me, it was an utter strangeness, an enforced span of contemplation that has left its mark on the remainder of my life.

## 27: Dissonance
*Madagascar*

It was nearing summer in the Northern Hemisphere when my boat at long last docked, but somewhere along the way we had slipped imperceptibly into the South, and – for now at least – winter was setting in around me for the second time in six months. I didn't know it then, but the days of European ships making this long journey home from Asia via Africa were numbered; already the Arctic in September was nearly ice-free, and soon its beleaguered icy canvasses would be gone forever, the grip of its ancient freeze retreating sufficiently all summer long for direct shipments to shave weeks off the voyage from China to northern Europe by crossing its once impassable seas.

For now, though, Madagascar's major port of Toamasina was still flourishing on the back of imports and exports facilitated by these passing ships. It was there that I abandoned my hitch-hike aboard the freighter, and tasted again the bitter-sweet reality of dry land and human civilisation. This was my first experience of Africa proper, an outpost on the eastern edge of the world's fourth-largest island, a dissonant mix of beautiful beaches and sparkling shark-infested seas alongside the ugly grey roads and buildings of modernity's pox. Even in the autumn, late May, it was a not unpleasant twenty five degrees, and as I walked further into the city I was met with more pleasing sights, sounds and scents as an exotic medley of spices exuded from the bustling market stalls. In a town indeed rooted in trade, the air hummed with a lovely language curious to my unaccustomed ear, but quite impossible for my sea-weary cognition to comprehend. Fortunately for me, the more familiar French was spoken alongside the tuneful Malagasy tongue.

Nearly three times the size of Great Britain, Madagascar nonetheless boasted an astounding range of climates and variegated living beings. For eighty-eight million years before the arrival of man, the island existed in complete isolation, and the magic of evolution worked wonders in the form of tens of thousands of plants and animals seen nowhere else in the world. Around ninety per cent of its flora and fauna once were endemic, making this an unparalleled paradise of biodiversity surely deserving of the most reverential and awestruck respect. By the time I had arrived, ninety per cent of the original forest had been cut down, and nearly all of the remainder would soon be gone, even the protected National Parks struggling to survive as unnaturally secluded pockets of life. The lemur, the most famous Madagascan animal, was already in dire danger then, with many of its hundred or so sub-species already having been driven to extinction by habitat loss. It wasn't difficult, as in so many such situations I'd seen, for me to guess why.

When the French finally withdrew in 1960, they left a land crippled by colonial exploitation; in spite of the rich natural splendour that surrounded them its people lived in a half-developed limbo that left them struggling to live fulfilling lives by either traditional or modern means. As a weary inland train brought me slowly into the capital, the world I saw around me was one stripped of its ancient African beauty in favour of an alien agricultural desert. Slash-and-burn, which had consumed much of the lost forest over the previous half-century, was going on apace, with some of the impoverished people desperate to cash in their un-costed and invaluable natural 'assets' for more profitable cattle and coffee plantations. Could they be blamed?

Perhaps in part, but the lion's share of the responsibility for this perverse atrocity of destruction – one by no means unique to this uniquely biodiverse land – must surely lie with those great ships such as the one I had arrived on, that greedily swarmed upon the port like wasps to a pot of honey, lapping up the island's treasures as if the supply would never fail. From vanilla to fish, cloves to coal and precious metals, all were for the taking, ripped unsympathetically from land and sea: a rape of Nature, right before my eyes. And somehow they believed that Nature wouldn't bite us back!

Antananarivo, like almost every major city in those days, was aspiring to be something that it wasn't meant to be: high-rising and modern, though the trend towards concrete, tarmac and bill-boards shouting about shopping was by no means as far advanced as in many other places I'd seen. Long gone, alas, were the traditional structures Madagascans used to build out of wood, reeds and grass – all entirely renewable and potentially sustainable local resources. But many quite charming, well-built French-era structures still adorned the capital, not to mention the splendid palaces that crowned the busy city's beautiful centre, albeit beautified by tree-lined avenues of a distinctly French feel. Nor, though, had the tradition of painful inequality that once separated noble and common classes disappeared; now it was the monetarily wealthy who occupied the characterful, spacious dwellings of the superior districts, while the poor were crammed into more hastily-erected ever-sprawling suburbs. They remained, both in geographical locality and in political power, very much on the periphery.

The dire state of this precious country, in which both culture and nature were severely under strain, became less of a surprise to me the more I learned of its rocky post-colonial road. The first president of an independent Madagascar was deposed after a decade or so for being too close to the French; his immediate successors lasted days, weeks or months before suffering death or deposition at the hands of rival powers. The country became painfully dependent upon unsustainable and unreliable sources of economic growth, and the 1970s oil crisis pushed it further into poverty. But it was the International Monetary Fund and the World Bank, big bullies that used to go about in those days holding countries to ransom over money, that insisted on liberalisation of the marketplace and privatisation of industries and services, increasing foreign trade and at the same time slashing state subsidies and pushing the poorest into greater desperation.

Material poverty is a great misery for those who struggle to survive, but at least for those lucky enough to have a meaningful job I found that a healthy and happy life was being lived amidst the poor. Many were free from the mixed blessing of electricity and the curse of private motor vehicles, neither of which presented much of a problem for the welcoming and hospitable people I met. Finding vegetarian food was no difficulty in a land where most people ate meat only on special occasions, to the benefit of their own health and the environment but primarily because of its expense. The rice paddies that surrounded the city must have brought their own greenhouse gas emissions, but three million people must needs be fed.

Perhaps it was feeding our growing population that doomed us in the end – perhaps the famous Malthus was right. Yet that's not how it seemed to me, looking down over the rambling rooftops from the great hill atop the city. It wasn't the vegetarian, electricity-deprived multitudes eking out a living in suburban shanty-towns that were destroying the future viability of our planet. Rather, it was amidst the sprinkling of supermarkets and bright, glitzy shops on the wealthier side of town that the real problem lay.

## 28: Charge
*Across southern Africa*

It was with some regret that I set out again to sea, and left the magical island and its comforting solidarity in exchange for days and nights sliding across the empty waves. This time, though, my journey was to be much shorter than before, and it wasn't long I had to wait for the hazy coast of Africa proper to shimmer onto my horizon, bright and new, and slowly but surely to magnify from tentative image to undeniable reality. So I came, at length, to the continent from which we all descended, to the mysterious land that caps the Old World's southern tip, to the sweltering sun-baked coast of South Africa.

I didn't stay long in the port of Durban, whose ugly urban architecture, archetypical of the modern age, I need not describe again to you who have heard me complain of so many similar cities. Africa's most advanced railway network soon had me chugging away from the shore, content not to see the sea again for a little while. And the prospect of almost an entire continent unexplored lured me onwards, not so much into the 'Heart of Darkness' as into the heart of the human story, with all its beauty and all its painful weaknesses. For if there was an Eden, was it not here? If once there was perfection in human existence, did it not sound as a note amidst the harmony of these other wonders of Nature, the first to be named? Such was the promise of Africa, whose southernmost slopes now slid past my window,

217

whose roads and rails could carry me to so many cultures and peoples of whom I knew not. The way home lay over a land less familiar to me than any other, about as far from England as it is possible to be and yet stamped with marks of British interference almost everywhere I looked.

Before heading north, I turned south, briefly, to cross a wide open veldt that hosted animals I'd only imagined, through diverse districts of peoples, each with their own tongues and traditions. The joy of Slow Travel was that I could see them all, albeit briefly. The cities may have been westernised, or more accurately colonised by capitalism, but the rural parts still hosted many traditional dwellers. A large proportion of the country's twenty percent who didn't profess to be Christian could be found here, still holding to their ancient beliefs, born out of the very soil of Africa, and I saw them enact their rituals, spilling the blood of animals to bring ancestral blessings. Such practices saddened me, certainly, but could I really claim the right to contradict a way of life and system of beliefs that had evolved here over the course of ten thousand years? At least these people were thankful for and careful with their meat, which was alas the mainstay of most South African meals, unlike those in the modern towns where it was an off-the-shelf commodity given little thought. To these people it was precious, to be eaten sparingly alongside grains and wild nuts and fruits. And it was not in the traditional villages that an imminent water shortage was big news, where water has always been gratefully received and carefully managed, but in Cape Town where rumours that the taps might run dry had sent the owners of golf courses, luxury swimming pools and flushing toilets into a panic.

There was one place in particular I could not resist visiting, though it took some time to find somebody able to take me there. The Karoo plains hosted little life and few, scattered farms, high in the north-west and as far away from the noise and the lights of the city as one could be on dry land. There the days are scorching, and nights can be bitter cold, not blanketed by cloud. There I found an utter peace, natural and primordial, in the silent evening beneath the waking stars. And there they shone, not spoiled in their celestial show by any foul orange oozes that mankind spills over other skies. No computers, no confounded machinations such as mobile telephones or petrol cars could be brought there: nothing that could disturb the inky blackness, the utter silence in which it was possible to listen and to dream – and to hear even the whispers of unseen distant worlds, with the right equipment.

This was the South African part of the Square Kilometre Array, a huge expanse of radio receivers split across the Southern Hemisphere, and intended to tune in eventually to signals fifty times less powerful that any other radio telescope could detect. Looking for life in the void beyond the heavens; peering out from one of the most lifeless expanses on Earth. When I saw it, the telescope wasn't yet complete, and I admit to mixed emotions regarding its construction. This was a project to pile nearly two hundred huge metal dishes into an area that had known the quiet of endless ages, and in the process would inevitably endanger the habitat of those few species that did still there wander through the dark. Radio quiet seemed refreshing indeed in those days when all the world was filling up with noise and endless gossip charging back and forth along invisible channels that one could not escape. But it was being imposed so that this telescope, when operational, could gather more information per second than that carried by all the traffic of the world wide web, stored on supercomputers sitting isolated in their underground Faraday cages and gobbling up megawatts of power in a country that still derived four-fifths of its energy from coal.

The local people, though perhaps they'd benefited from a little extra science funding in their schools, expressed worries about the collapse of the agriculture that clung on amidst the sparsity and the cutting off of their communities from global communications networks. The government-endorsed land-grab from white sheep farmers was painfully reminiscent of the policies of post-colonial Zimbabwe nearby. The nub of the matter for me was this though, speaking as a physicist and one-time astronomer myself: was listening so carefully to the stars for answers to the big questions posed by theoreticians and philosophers in their steel towers far away really worth invading this huge expanse of unique countryside? We've only got one Earth, as we all so bitterly know now. Why waste all its resources looking up for something else?

Yet I must admit that the astronomers' impact was like the erecting of a mole-hill next to a mountain when set against the damage done by other big colonialist industries in Africa. It began with the Europeans and their 'enlightened' culture; it hadn't gone away with the arrival of the capitalist empire. The raping of Africa for its jewels went on apace in South Africa, still more so than in Madagascar: here iron, coal, gold and diamonds were being ripped in vast quantities from deep and dangerous mines where only the poorest in their desperation risked their lives to labour. And what for, all this plunder? Only trinkets and trivialities next to Nature's universally unmatchable splendour.

## 29: Elemental
*Into the Heart of Africa*

Cecil Rhodes once dreamed of a railway that would run right up the length of Africa, from Cape Town to Cairo through a long line of conjoined British colonies. One by one, most of the necessary tribes and kingdoms of ancient Africa had fallen into Britain's grip by the end of the nineteenth century, but the scheme was scuppered by German East Africa, which remained a thorn in the British Empire's side until the First World War, then by the Great Depression, the Second World War and the process of decolonisation that then ensued. Thus the dream went unfulfilled, but the British did complete the stretch from South Africa to Tanzania, half way up the continent on the Eastern side, albeit with a large gap between there and Sudan, where another line linked up to Egypt. It was on this great railway that I embarked, one fine afternoon towards the end of Southern Hemisphere autumn, and prepared to make my journey back northwards through the secret heart of Africa.

Only the famous 'Blue Train' did the journey from Cape Town to Tanzania in one stretch, a train that only the elite could afford to ride. My journey I took more gradually, changing trains regularly to ride alongside more ordinary Africans and experience something of the urban conurbations separated by such splendid stretches of countryside. Thus, from Pretoria, South Africa's posher capital (and much less dangerous than Johannesburg) to Bulawayo in Zimbabwe, to avoid

222

the slick blue carriages with their solid gold taps and unappetising offerings of luxury, I was obliged to leave the train and board a bus to Botswana, thence catching an unhurried and somewhat rustic service, with more staff than passengers, which being slower gave me more opportunity to witness the changing landscape about me and the celebrated fauna living out their lives beside the roads and the tracks.

Zimbabwe was a name of infamy in those times, when memories of the lately deposed dictator-come-president Mugabe and his famously inept policies that may have shortened millions of lives were still fresh in many minds. Having had a currency so rattled by inflation that the wheelbarrows carrying mounds of cash were worth more than the dollars they contained and a Land Reform Programme that sought to dispossess ex-colonial farmers but in the process brought millions to the brink of starvation, the Zimbabwe I witnessed was a country just beginning to stumble back onto its feet. The new government wasn't necessarily much better than its predecessor, and though few would have welcomed the return of Mr Mugabe, perhaps there was something of the man that was missed by a people that had once idolised their freedom-fighter champion of independence. The spirit of rejuvenation that he had once espoused had converted 'Southern Rhodesia' with its racialist rule into a free Zimbabwe governed by a long-oppressed majority. A new rejuvenation was what the country sorely needed, still dependent on tobacco exports as its major industry, still clearing forests to heat the tobacco barns and still suffering from elections essentially controlled by the ruling party.

I was not a common sight, in those days, as a European traveller, in a land where the tourist industry had long since collapsed and to which – thankfully from my environmentalist perspective – very few airlines bothered to fly. But there had been days when the British were a rarer sight still, most notably in 1855 when the intrepid David Livingstone first set a European eye on Africa's brightest hidden gem, the world's biggest waterfall, and renamed it Victoria Falls. The railway from Zimbabwe to Zambia still climbed through the once dark and mysterious forests that flanked the great impassable Zambesi River, crossing by a vast Victorian bridge, and it was well worth pausing there to be taken aback looking upon the incredible sight of what in the indigenous Tonga tongue was called the 'Smoke that Thunders'. Unimaginable gallons of clear water, toppling from a rocky cliff with an unimaginably voluminous sound: this was indeed a wonder of Nature, a grand spectacle whose proportions had to be seen to be comprehended.

East Africa is a land of scrambling rivers, whose treacherous courses, impossible to follow, give a sense of leading towards some lost treasure: staircases to paradise that defeat all those who try to climb. An element of Eden, which was said to be bounded by four just such rivers, could be seen amidst those forests. To the West of Zambia flows the Zambesi, to the north trickles a tributary to the great Congo, their courses cutting across boundaries of artificially drawn-up states. The rivers were valued there, certainly: for their beauty; for the burgeoning tourist industry that they continued to bring to the old 'Northern Rhodesia'; and, alas, for the potential hydropower to be had by damming them.

Zambia was a beautiful and relatively unspoiled country; its huge twenty-fold population growth of the previous century had largely occurred in the cities, where nearly half the people lived, leaving large parts of the countryside sparsely inhabited. Yet there was only one element that the big powers there had been focussed on for decades: atomic number 29, Copper. As a result of this, Zambia had become a good example of a country heavily influenced by the sway of capitalist markets. When the copper price was high, the money rolled in and the rich especially flourished; when the copper price fell, the money brought in by mining dried up and the poor especially floundered. In Lusaka, the people talked about increasing diversification of the economy, but the majority of exports were still those of element 29, and this was certainly not the place to be advocating hopes for a world with one hundred per cent recycling and the phasing out of mining for metals.

Another train brought me to another country, up through the picturesque flat pains of the Sarengeti into Tanzania, where the railway ran out. Here were Africa's largest lakes – including Victoria (the etymology of which is again not difficult to fathom) and Tanganyika, the deepest, known for its unique fish – and Africa's tallest mountain, Kilimanjaro. It was an astonishing sight. My slow travel had brought me through a truly foreign land, one where sometimes fatal superstitions still lingered amidst the majority rural population, where more than a hundred ancient languages were spoken, but where more than a third of the countryside was protected for conservation. It' wasn't difficult to see why. Erupting shards of earth, imploding pools of water, untainted air beneath the fiery autumn sun: all the elements were there in their purest form. A 'heart of darkness' indeed this was not, I reflected as the last red rays of sunlight set the western sky alight. This was the crowning star of Nature's primordial display.

## 30: Worship
*Journey's End*

I could not know, as I scrambled through the suburbs and savannah of Kenya and Ethiopia while May slipped into June of 2019, that my long Slow Travel – over a year by then in duration – was so soon, so hurriedly, to come to a close. Since that sunny spring day when I had set out from Britain to see for myself the sorry state of a changed and battered world, and its ills social and environmental, I had criss-crossed Europe, Asia, North America and Africa. The beautiful continents of South America and Australasia and the white wilderness of Antarctica, of which I can only dream, it was my fate never to see. Now, fifty years hence, there is likely little left there worth seeing.

Back then, we still had hope. The forests were depleted but not destroyed beyond hope of recovery; the deserts had begun expanding but not without hope of arrest. So much of the coal and the oil that had brought us into this mess was still in the ground; we thought that this would be enough. But we hadn't reckoned on the fateful power of two dangerous adversities: the unquenchable reality of human greed, and the unstoppable force of nature's reaction once unleashed. Both these hard truths were about to sweep over us. It would take years for us to come to terms with it, but the fact remained: very soon, there would be no way back.

In those days, Kenya seemed exotic, with its humid tropical climate and its cooler, tranquil savanna

227

hosting all the 'big five' game animals that thoughtless trophy-hunters liked to kill for sport or cash – lion, leopard, elephant, buffalo and rhino. The Serengeti migration of the blue wildebeest, a fantastic sight to behold for one fortunate enough to arrive at the right time, was said to be one of the seven 'Natural Wonders of Africa'. Much effort was being spent preserving all these glorious species, each individual a splendid spectacle of nature's fine design, and all endangered under the corrupt stewardship of mankind.

The influence of China, which I saw all around me from the new railway line sporting swish Chinese trains to the Chinese-funded buildings springing up like warts upon the city skylines, hadn't helped. It was China that had the biggest appetite for 'medicinal' animal body parts, and drove the blind machine of the capitalist marketplace towards the illegal destruction of elephant and rhino to meet demand. Nor did it help that the mostly agrarian populations of both Kenya and Ethiopia – where four fifths of the workforce were agricultural workers – required more and more land, farmed in less traditional and less nature-friendly ways than before, and were putting increasing pressure on areas not explicitly protected as habitat. On the other hand, it might have been supposed that a growing tourist industry would be a means of saving all that beauty that I myself was captivated by, if only for foreigners to gaup at and photograph.

But in truth it was not the Chinese medicine-hunters or the Kenyan and Ethiopian locals that tolled the death knell for those wild wonders of Africa's ancient heart, but the tourists – with their kerosene-guzzling aeroplanes, their meaty diets and their swanky hotels. Kenyans and Ethiopians had been living here since the dawn of humanity itself, in a many millennia long coexistence with the big mammals. Within the space of a generation they would all be gone, not because of hunting but because of climatic change that the locals, whose meagre supplies of electricity were almost met by geothermal and hydroelectric carbon-free means, had nothing to do with.

A dusty bus brought be from the beautiful lakes of northern Kennya high into the heart of Ethiopia, and up into the scorching lands where heavily-logged forest retreated into desert. How pilgrims managed to walk to the Holy City of Axum in such heat I know not, but braving such inclement heat was worth it for what I was there to see. This ancient site of human habitation was home – so it was rumoured – to the oldest relic of the Abrahamic religions, the original Ark of the Covenant described in the Old Testament.

Whether the story of one of Solomon's sons carrying the Ark here three millennia ago was true, and the small chapel beside the great Ethiopian Church cathedral really did hold the Ark, it was difficult to tell. Nobody was allowed inside to see – not even the patriarch of the Ethiopian church – except for a wizened old monk. But this holy site of worship, the centrepiece of a country supposedly the second ever to adopt Christianity officially, in 333 AD, was nonetheless breath-taking to

229

behold. The Ethiopian Church is distinct from any other, and certainly seemed to hold the Old Testament particularly close to its heart, with its Jewish dietary customs and 250 days per year of fasting from meat and dairy products – perhaps not accidentally also the best thing that any climate-conscious individual could have done to avert the doom that was coming upon the world.

But the world, by and large, did not worship the God of the Old Testament or the New, and was not much concerned with fasting. It worshiped three gods: greed, growth and money, and when in its distress it came to cry to them for help it received no response. It was on my way from Axum, crossing the straggling saplings that made up the eastern side of Africa's version of the 'Great Green Wall' intended to stymie the Sahara, that I heard the news. My Slow Travel through Sudan would have to be cut short; I now needed desperately to return home.

Khartoum to Cairo by ferry and train isn't quick, nor the boat back to Europe from the mouth of the Nile, that great long river that I'd followed all the way from the heart of Africa. Many more splendid sights I saw pass by, but had little time to stop. The days now seemed a burden to me; the hours that had slipped so easily by now dragged like heavy weights. I longed to see my home again – that precious isle of rolling hills and winding lanes and sunlight-sprinkled woods – before it was gone, for ever. For the permafrost was melting now; methane belching into the sky. A hidden line had been crossed, the dam was broken and there was no hope of halting the flood. And sackcloth, fasting and repentance were not, it seemed, going to be part of the world's response. Heightening tensions had at last spilled over, panic was ensuing: for that same day, war had been declared.

And that was that: the end of my journey of discovery; the end of the world that was. You don't need me to tell you about the wreckage that now remains.

Lightning Source UK Ltd.
Milton Keynes UK
UKHW022304070223
416603UK00012B/240

9 781739 135720